THE GOSPEL OF JOHN
SET FREE

Studies in
Judaism and Christianity

*Exploration of Issues in the
Contemporary Dialogue Between
Christians and Jews*

Editor in Chief for
Stimulus Books
Lawrence Boadt

Editors
Lawrence Boadt, CSP
Rabbi Leon Klenicki
Kevin A. Lynch, CSP
Rev. Dennis McManus
Dr. Ann Riggs
Rabbi Leonard Schoolman
Dr. Elena Procario-Foley
Michael Kerrigan, CSP

A STIMULUS BOOK

THE GOSPEL OF JOHN
SET FREE

Preaching without Anti-Judaism

George M. Smiga

A STIMULUS BOOK

PAULIST PRESS ♦ NEW YORK ♦ MAHWAH, NJ

Cover design by Sharyn Banks
Book design by Lynn Else and Theresa M. Sparacio

Library of Congress Cataloging-in-Publication Data

Smiga, George M., 1948–
    The Gospel of John set free : preaching without anti-Judaism / George M. Smiga.
        p. cm.
    Includes bibliographical references.
    ISBN-13: 978-0-8091-4457-0 (alk. paper)
    1. Bible. N.T. John—Criticism, interpretation, etc. 2. Judaism (Christian theology)—History of doctrines—Early church, ca. 30–600. 3. Jews in the New Testament. 4. Bible. N.T. John—Homiletical use. 5. Catholic Church. Lectionary for Mass (U.S.) 6. Bible. N.T. John—Liturgical lessons, English. I. Title.
    BS2615.6.J44S65 2008
    226.5'06—dc22

                                                                              2007051111

Published by Paulist Press
997 Macarthur Boulevard
Mahwah, New Jersey 07430

www.paulistpress.com

Printed and bound in the
United States of America

Contents

Readings from the Gospel of John in Cycle B

Readings from the Gospel of John in Cycle C

Foreword

The Stimulus Foundation came into existence in 1977, founded by the late Helga Croner, for the purpose of producing scholarly publications aimed at increasing mutual understanding between Christians and Jews. More than fifty volumes have been published on a large number of important and often sensitive issues. These books were written by some of the most distinguished scholars in the Jewish and Christian communities. They have found a wide and receptive audience. Paulist Press has been honored to be an active partner in this significant undertaking.

With this first book in the *Gospel Set Free* series, the Stimulus Foundation offers a new and very practical tool for the dialogue between Jews and Christians. It deals in concrete ways with the proper presentation of Judaism in the books of the New Testament. The series is written by highly qualified scholars but at a very popular level. It is intended for both Christian leaders — preachers, homiletic professors, teachers, and religious educators — and for Christian and Jewish groups that wish to meet together in dialogue. Each book in the series reveals both the appreciation of Judaism by the early Christian community and how the community's simultaneous disparagement of Judaism set the stage for so much of the anti-Semitism in the centuries that followed.

I wish to express the gratitude of the Stimulus Board to Rabbi Leon Klenicki and Rev. Dennis McManus for their diligent and dedicated editorial work on this project. We hope *The Gospel Set Free* will make a significant contribution to improved Jewish and Christian understanding.

Rev. Kevin A. Lynch, CSP
President Emeritus, The Stimulus Foundation

Editors' Preface

This book marks a kind of revolution in the church's reading of the gospel. For here, as never before in a concentrated way, the reader is invited to consider how to read the gospels and epistles of the New Testament *free of anti-Jewish sentiment*. While there are numerous studies by the most eminent of scholars on the problem of anti-Judaism and anti-Semitism in the New Testament, no single series has ever proposed a continuous commentary on a given book of the Christian scriptures from this point of view. *The Gospel of John Set Free*, then, intends to change the way in which pastors and teachers present the texts of the Sunday scripture readings in particular so that Christians may understand not only how completely these writings were formed in a Jewish surrounding, but also how routinely Christians have come to read them in an *anti-Jewish* way.

The impetus for this project might be said to come from the concentration that the late pope, John Paul II, brought to bear on the relationship of the Roman Catholic Church to Jews and Judaism worldwide. For in his twenty-six-plus years as pope, he was the first to visit a synagogue since the days of the apostles. He readily admitted—as his remarkable speech of October 31, 1997, records—that the Catholic tradition, especially as found in the some of the fathers of the church, set the groundwork for a deeply anti-Jewish reading of the New Testament that repeatedly became an excuse for the indifference of Christians toward Jews, culminating in the unspeakable evil of the Shoah. No doubt in part because of his own unique rearing with Jewish friends and neighbors in his boyhood Poland, John Paul II was the first pope in two thousand years to address so profoundly the conflicts that have troubled the church's relationship with the Jews.

The results of his efforts are overwhelming. Now in Europe, North and South America, bishops and rabbis find themselves in an ongoing dialogue with each other. Catholic parishes and Jewish congregations are seen to befriend each other, even to the point where entire Catholic dioceses in the United States have renewed their religious and social-service practices in boldly crafted "covenants of friendship," such as between the Roman Catholic Diocese of Albany and the local Jewish community (see *The Rochester Agreement,* by Dr. Eugene Fisher, Rabbi Leon Klenicki, and Dr. Joseph G. Kelly [New York: ADL, 1996], concluded between the Roman Catholic Diocese of Rochester, the Rochester Board of Rabbis, and the Jewish Community Federation of Rochester). Such innovative approaches to a sharing of faith and the service of those in need would have been nearly unthinkable until our own day.

Much, however, remains to be done in the education of both pastoral-staff members and believing Christians generally in understanding what it means to read the gospels free of anti-Judaism. Perhaps it is wise to distinguish early on the difference between the two key phrases of *anti-Judaism* and *anti-Semitism.* The former term describes a theological or religious belief that Judaism is to be opposed or at least dismissed, usually on the grounds that Christianity has surpassed it as the new and only covenant that God has with his chosen people.

In anti-Judaism, Jews are seen as the killers of Christ, the Messiah, and as blind followers of the Mosaic Law, which cannot lead to salvation. The later term, *anti-Semitism,* denotes a specific set of racist beliefs made popular in the mid- to late-nineteenth century by European race theorists, who maintained that Jews were physically, morally, and culturally inferior as a racial group to all Aryan peoples. The tragedy pointed out by John Paul II is that anti-*Judaism* often enabled the uninhibited application of anti-*Semitism* in social and legal policies of the twentieth century, and with appalling results. Christians whose consciences had been numbed, as it were, with anti-Judaism either in the church's liturgy or her preaching on the gospel could only challenge the anti-Semitism of the Nazis, Fascists, and the Communists with great difficulty. In a sense, then, anti-Judaism became the theological excuse for many Christians to permit one form or another of anti-Semitic thought, speech, or action. As recent history has shown, here also the results have been overwhelming.

Nevertheless, it must be asked over and over again: "How was it that the church's reading of the Christian scriptures became so

deeply infected with anti-Jewish sentiment?" The answer is not difficult to find when one notices that any attempt to read the gospels or
epistles *outside of their Jewish contexts* will certainly result in at least
a misunderstanding of the literal meaning of these texts. Throughout
the patristic era in particular, it was common to find commentaries by
non-Jewish authors who found themselves in conflict with local
Jewish communities. The result was predictable: an exposition of
scripture that fostered what Jules Isaac would call "the teaching of
contempt," that is, the devaluation of Judaism by its being made into
the object of a misplaced hatred related to the death of Jesus. The
reading of the gospels outside of their original Jewish context—as
stories by Jews, for Jews, told within Judaism and based upon the
foundations of the teaching of one who allowed himself to be called
"Rabbi"—is one of the principal causes of the anti-Judaism that
resulted. For only when the reader fully appreciates the fact that
Judaism, as the expression of God's long-standing covenant with his
chosen people, is the basis that gives meaning to the life, death, and
teaching of Jesus, only then can a new appreciation of the Jewish
foundation of the Christian tradition be realized.

Nor should we fear that such a method for the reading of the
New Testament is out of step with modern scripture studies: Nothing
could be further from the truth. The same movement in biblical studies that helped establish the correct literal meaning of texts through
historical and form criticism has, in fact, helped scholars to understand that an appreciation of the Jewish context and meaning of
gospel stories is not only essential for a proper theological understanding of the text, but that no literal sense of the text can ever be
proposed that is not built on its Jewish background.

This, too, is a revolution of sorts. For how many times in the
history of Christian exegesis have commentators been sure of their
unholy footing in misreading the gospel in an anti-Jewish or even an
anti-Semitic way? Positive that they have understood the literal sense
of the text apart from its Jewish content, even fathers of the church
such as Augustine and John Chrysostom have drawn conclusions
that, in the end, seem only remotely related to the apparent intention
of the evangelists. This present series of books is proposing that
unless and until the Jewish context and elements of each New
Testament passage are understood, then the literal sense of the text
remains out of reach.

In this series, each biblical story is discussed by the volume author to help the reader understand what Jewish elements may be present in the story and to explain their relationship to the further revelations of Jesus. This approach is not intended to change the text (a sacred one) but instead to highlight the unique vocation of Jesus in relation to the Judaism of the first century. The results are always enlightening, but occasionally quite striking—as when the volume authors discuss who is responsible for the death of Jesus.

Perhaps the most unusual characteristic of this series is its use of rabbinic parallels to the texts chosen for commentary. As often as possible, the editors have provided the reader with citations to rabbinic literature that, paralleling the gospel text in question, help to illuminate the Jewish background and meaning of the text. In addition, Talmudic texts are also referenced for whatever light they may shed on the meaning of the gospel. As well, each commentary has been subdivided by the editors, with added questions for discussion and reflection in order to promote the use of these books in pastoral and educational settings. Finally, each volume offers the reader a short bibliography of resources that can provide greater depth to the questions raised in the commentary. For further reading in the many references to the Mishnah within this series, Jacob Neusner's *The Mishnah: A New Translation* (New Haven: Yale University Press, 1988), with its helpful introduction and extensive index and citation charts, is recommended.

A final point must be stated clearly. Much of present-day scholarship maintains that the texts of the gospels and other New Testament compositions are, in fact, at least anti-Jewish if not also anti-Semitic. It has been the assumption of *this* series that this is *not* the case, since the authors of the New Testament were clearly Jewish and, in many cases, wrote their works as Jews for Jews within the context of Jewish theology and the following of Jesus. However, it is equally true that New Testament texts have been frequently used and abused for anti-Semitic purposes, helping to create an ideology of hatred toward the Jewish people through the centuries, culminating in the Shoah. The recent statement of the 2001 Pontifical Biblical Commission entitled, *The Jewish People and Their Sacred Scriptures in the Christian Bible,* explains this best when it states:

> Real anti-Jewish feeling, that is, an attitude of contempt, hostility and persecution of the Jews as Jews, is not found

in any New Testament text and is incompatible with its teaching. What is found are reproaches addressed to certain categories of Jews for religious reasons, as well as polemical texts to defend the Christian apostolate against Jews who oppose it. (¶ 87)

At the same time, the commission warns that many of the passages of the New Testament have been used provocatively as a pretext for anti-Jewish sentiment. Its summary statement of this problem is well worth our reflection. Referring to the misreading and manipulative use of the New Testament for anti-Jewish purposes, the commission writes:

> To avoid mistakes of this kind, it must be kept in mind that the New Testament polemical texts, even those expressed in general terms, have to do with concrete historical contexts and are never meant to be applied to Jews of all times and places merely because they are Jews. The tendency to speak in general terms, to accentuate the adversaries' negative side, and to pass over the positive in silence, failure to consider their motivations and their ultimate good faith, these are characteristics of all polemical language throughout antiquity, and are no less evident in Judaism and primitive Christianity against all kinds of dissidents. (¶ 87).

In short, while a close reading of the New Testament in its Jewish context will help to educate Christians as to the Jewish background of Jesus and his disciples, such a reading does not reveal anti-Jewish or anti-Semitic intent on the part of the biblical authors. But just as surely, this new way of reading for the Judaism in the New Testament text exposes as a lie any attempt to use such a text for the purpose of condemning, replacing, or otherwise discounting the ultimate value of Judaism to the salvation of the entire world.

In the chapters that follow, the central commentary has been written by Rev. George Smiga, while the rabbinic commentary and notes, as well as the discussion questions at the end of the volume, have been provided by the editors. Father Smiga's insights are extremely illuminating, often dispelling old and biased readings of many familiar gospel stories. His scholarship in New Testament studies — and on the

Gospel of John in particular—has made him an authority on the topic we are examining. But most of all it is Father Smiga's ability to relate the problem of anti-Judaism in the reading of John to pastoral teams and, indeed, to every Catholic in the pew on Sunday that makes this volume the success that it is. Each of his reflections on the Gospel readings is well worth the time that an individual or a pastoral team can give to it.

The biblical texts cited are those to be found in the special translation of the lectionary for Mass used in the Roman Catholic Church in the dioceses of the United States of America, but they can also be found in the liturgical reading cycles of many Christian churches, though in different translations.

Rabbi Leon Klenicki
Rev. Dennis D. McManus
Series Co-Editors

Introduction to the Gospel of John

THE GOSPELS AS BOTH FAITH AND HISTORY

If the problem of anti-Judaism within the Gospel of John is to be adequately addressed, the nature of the gospel writings must be appreciated. Although many Christian believers remain unaware of the fact, the gospels are not biographies of Jesus. Their purpose is not to present what Jesus said and did as literal history. They are primarily documents of faith, encouraging the reader to accept Jesus as the risen Lord. The Gospel of John (20:31) states this purpose clearly when it asserts that the signs within it "are written so that you may come to believe that Jesus is the Messiah, the Son of God, and that through believing you may have life in his name."

This does not mean that the gospels are documents describing imaginary events without historical basis. Jesus lived, taught, healed, suffered, and died. All this was part of human history. The memories of Jesus' mission were passed down within the Christian communities and became part of the gospels. However, the process by which these events were included within the New Testament writings was both creative and flexible.

The Roman Catholic Church officially described this process in 1964 when the Pontifical Biblical Commission issued "An Instruction on the Historical Truth of the Gospels." In that document the commission outlined three stages in the development of the gospels. *Stage one* is the life and death of Jesus, which is the historical basis of our faith. The resurrection marks the beginning of *stage two*. In this period the apostles began to proclaim Jesus as the risen Lord. The commission notes that in this proclamation the apostles *interpreted* the words and deeds of Jesus from stage one in the fuller light that they received after the resurrection. Moreover, they *adapted* the message to meet the needs of the people to whom they spoke. *Stage three* identifies the process by which the oral preaching of the apostles was

1

written down to become our present gospels. In this stage the sacred authors were free to shape the material further so that it suited their particular purposes and the situations of their communities.

As is clear from this three-stage development, the words and deeds of Jesus were reshaped by both early Christian preachers and the evangelists in order to better suit their primary aim of spreading the good news of Jesus' death and resurrection. In this process much of the historical material from Jesus' ministry and passion was preserved. But it was reworked in the fuller light of the resurrection and by including perspectives that would more specifically relate to the particular audience being addressed. Therefore, as we approach any gospel text, it is essential to be aware that what lies before us is a *mixture* of historical material from stage one together with the insights and issues of later Christian preachers and writers.

There is an unfortunate tendency in some circles to limit the value of the text only to those portions that can be traced back to the actual words and deeds of Jesus (stage one). This is a narrow and extreme approach. The later interpretations of the words and deeds of Jesus by the apostles (stage two) are essential perspectives, presenting Jesus' ministry in light of the fuller understanding of the resurrection. The theological viewpoints of the evangelists who shaped the material in light of their own situation (stage three) add to the richness and diversity of the faith proclamation. The biblical text has been formed through all three stages of development. It is this complete text that the church holds as inspired by the action of the Holy Spirit. Therefore, the process by which the gospels came to be should not be used to claim that one stage is more important than another. The entire text is the word of God.

Yet as we face the difficult problems in the Gospel of John, it will be important to recognize that some of the presentations of Jews and Judaism within the gospels do not reflect the life and ministry of Jesus but arise rather from situations that Christian preachers and writers faced in subsequent decades of the first century. The span of time from the ministry of Jesus (stage one) to a written text (stage three) varies from gospel to gospel. For the Gospel of John, the span is some sixty years. A tremendous amount of change in attitude and circumstance can occur within that amount of time. We will see in the following pages how debates and conflicts in the community of John toward the end of the first century substantially affected the manner in which Jesus' ministry and his relationship to Judaism were presented. To say this in another way, the issues of stage three have influenced the manner in which the events and relationships of stage one have been narrated.

Recognizing the stages of gospel development and assigning the assertions of the text to the particular stages from which they arose will be an invaluable tool to us as we seek to understand the anti-Judaic potential in the Gospel of John. This approach will assist us in correcting false assumptions concerning Jesus' life and death and in appreciating the difficult issues that early believers in Christ faced as they began to separate from Judaism.

JUDAISM IN STAGE ONE OF THE GOSPEL TRADITION

During the life and ministry of Jesus (stage one), Judaism was a vibrant and complex form of religious expression. The spiritual power of Jewish convictions was evident in the variety of religious groups and movements. The Roman historian Josephus reports that during the first half of the first century CE, the chief Jewish groups were the Sadducees, the Pharisees, and the Essenes. His description of a fourth group is most likely to be identified with the Zealot movement.

There is limited knowledge concerning the exact beliefs and influence of these groups. The Sadducees, however, seemed to have drawn their membership from the Jewish aristocracy and exercised control over the Temple. The Pharisees were a reform movement, attempting to extend the sacredness of the Temple into everyday life. The Essenes formed an intense spiritual community that withdrew from society and dwelt in the Judean desert, probably at Qumran. The Zealots were determined to cleanse the land of Roman occupation and reestablish Israel as a community subject only to the authority of God. Names and allusions have come down to us from ancient sources that indicate there were other Jewish groups active at the time of Jesus. Although it is difficult to discover their beliefs and objectives, they are a further indication of the energy and creativity of Judaism during the first century.

ROMAN IMPERIALISM IN STAGE ONE
OF THE GOSPEL TRADITION

During the life and ministry of Jesus, the land of Israel was subject to the occupying power of the Roman Empire. Galilee was ruled by Antipas, the son of Herod the Great. Antipas ruled at the will of Rome and was responsible for paying tribute to the emperor and maintaining public order. Judea, which included the city of Jerusalem, was ruled by a governor appointed by the emperor. At the time of Jesus' death, that governor was Pontius Pilate.

Rome expected two things from its governors: that they keep the peace and collect the taxes. Governors who could not meet these expectations were quickly replaced. The number of Roman troops on Jewish soil was small compared to the population. Therefore, Roman governors, such as Pontius Pilate, achieved their aims through the control of the Jewish Temple leadership, particularly the Jewish high priest. The high priest during Jesus' ministry was Joseph Caiaphas. He was appointed by Pilate and would certainly be removed if he failed to assist the governor in his imperial objectives.

Through the arrangement between Pilate and Caiaphas, the day-to-day life of Jerusalem was governed by the high priest and his council. Yet Caiaphas was keenly aware that, when issues of public order or the collection of taxes were threatened, his position of authority was threatened as well. In other words, although Caiaphas exercised a good deal of control over the civic and religious issues that pertained to the everyday life of the Jewish populace, when issues touched upon the central interests of imperial Rome, he was forced to cooperate with the governor if he wished his authority to continue.

As we shall see, this forced alliance between the Roman governor and the Temple leadership must be borne in mind when the events of Jesus' death are examined. The involvement of the Temple authorities in Jesus' crucifixion was inextricably tied to the political situation that required the high priest and his council to defer to the interests of imperial Rome.

JESUS IN STAGE ONE OF THE GOSPEL TRADITION

There is a substantial consensus today among scholars that the historical Jesus was a faithful Jew. His ministry and his message of proclaiming the reign of God fit easily into the rich matrix of Judaism in the first century. As a rabbi, Jesus entered into debates over the interpretation of the Jewish law. There is, however, no compelling reason to conclude that Jesus opposed the law or rejected its value in any substantial way. The heated debates found in the gospels that reject certain Jewish customs and beliefs most likely did not originate with the historical Jesus. These disputes were a reflection of the issues of later Christian communities as they strove to establish their separate identities. For example, the question whether one should observe the Jewish Sabbath or food laws is better situated in the debates of Christian believers after the resurrection than in disputes during Jesus' ministry.

It is best, then, to picture the historical Jesus as observing the common religious practices of Judaism, conforming to the Jewish dietary expectations, honoring the Sabbath, worshiping in the Temple, and drawing deeply from the faith traditions of his ancestors. Parallels to most, if not all, of Jesus' teachings can be found in the Hebrew scriptures and in the message of other Jewish rabbis of his day. His proclamation of the reign of God and his message of love, mercy, and the forgiveness of sins were thoroughly Jewish. Although after his death and resurrection his disciples found their greatest success among Gentiles, it seems that Jesus himself envisioned his ministry as a movement within Judaism.

THE OPPONENTS OF JESUS AS PRESENTED IN THE GOSPELS

It is historically dubious that Jesus' ministry evoked universal skepticism or rejection from the Jews of his time. The conflicts between Jesus and other Jews in the gospels have been colored by the issues of later Christian communities. The evangelists were inclined to identify their opponents with the opponents of Jesus. Thus the opponents of stage three were often inserted into a narrative that was describing stage one. As a result, Jesus' opponents in the written gospels do not reflect the diversity of Jewish groups that were active during his ministry. The Essenes are never mentioned in the gospels. The Zealots are brought up once when one of the apostles, Simon, is identified as "the Zealot" (Luke 6:15). The Sadducees are mentioned nine times, most frequently in Matthew.

The gospels present the Pharisees as Jesus' chief opponents. They are mentioned eighty-eight times in the four gospels. Although there are some positive descriptions of them, most often they are pre-

sented in a negative light and in conflict with Jesus. They are frequently described as hypocrites, obsessed with the details of the law
and unconcerned with the burdens their teaching might impose on
others. Relying only on the description of the Pharisees that is present
within the gospels, one would conclude that they were the most
important Jewish group during Jesus' ministry and the one most
opposed to him. There are substantial reasons to believe that neither
of these conclusions is accurate.

In the early decades of the first century, the Pharisees were one
among many Jewish groups. When Jerusalem and its Temple were
destroyed in 70 CE by the Roman general, Titus, the status of Jewish
groups was dramatically altered. The Sadducees and Essenes did not
survive the war with Rome. The Pharisees, however, were able to
continue by creatively adapting to the new situation. In time, the
Pharisaic movement developed into what became rabbinic Judaism,
from which all major branches of contemporary Judaism trace their
lineage. The Pharisees attained prominence within Judaism only after
70 CE. With this prominence, they became the foil against which the
early Christian communities sought to define themselves. Therefore,
the hostility between Jesus and the Pharisees that we find in the
gospels is in large part a retrogression of the hostility between early
Christians and the Pharisees that took place after the destruction of
Jerusalem.

There are also compelling reasons to conclude that the teaching
of the historical Jesus was similar to that of the Pharisees. The
Pharisees promoted a belief in God as a loving Father. Unlike the
Sadducees, they believed in the resurrection of the dead. When we
examine rabbinic literature (which has evolved from Pharisaic roots)
we can identify the frequent use of parables, and several of these parables demonstrate striking similarities to those of Jesus. The *Sh'ma*
("Hear, O Israel, the Lord our God is Lord alone") was a central focus
of the rabbinic liturgy. The Golden Rule was the preeminent teaching
of Rabbi Hillel. Both of these traditions, honored by the Pharisees, are
employed by Jesus in Mark 12:29–31 to present the greatest commandment. These similarities strongly indicate that the Pharisees
were not Jesus' central opponents during his ministry nor did they
hold substantial disagreements with him during stage one of the
gospel tradition. This awareness is reflected in the 1985 statement of
the Vatican Commission for Religious Relations with the Jews

("Notes on the Correct Way to Present the Jews and Judaism in Preaching and Catechesis in the Roman Catholic Church," #19) when it asserts that an exclusively negative picture of the Pharisees is likely to be "inaccurate and unjust" and that Jesus was closer to the Pharisees than to other Jewish groups of his time.

By stage three of the gospel tradition, however, we face a radically altered landscape. The proclamation of Jesus as risen Lord and Messiah was begun by the early church. The Temple has been destroyed. The Pharisees have increased in influence, and substantial disagreements have developed between their claims for God's intentions and those of the early Christian communities. Therefore, as the stories of Jesus were committed to written form, these disagreements, conflicts, and attacks were read back into the narration of Jesus' words and deeds.

This adaptation of the gospel materials was advantageous to the evangelists. With the Pharisees serving as Jesus' chief opponents, the first readers of the gospels could draw a parallel between Jesus' situation and their own. Just as they believed that their disagreements with the Pharisees were following Jesus' will and purpose, early Christians could now find in the gospels a Jesus who was engaged in the same struggle. In this way, the Pharisees, who may well have played a rather small and harmonious role in the ministry of Jesus in stage one of the gospel tradition, emerge in the written gospels as Jesus' main rivals. They are the ones constantly opposing his teachings and even plotting his death. We shall find that this tendency to insert the opponents of later Christian communities into the gospel narratives has a direct connection to our understanding of the Gospel of John.

THE GOSPEL OF JOHN

The Gospel of John is generally believed to have been written during the 90s of the first century CE. This places it as the latest of the four gospels of the New Testament. The three earlier gospels (the Synoptics) share a substantial amount of material among them. John stands apart. Although John agrees with the Synoptics in several key ways, this Gospel has access to information that is independent of the earlier gospels and that has been elaborated in ways peculiarly its own.

A Choice for Jesus in a Dualistic World

All four gospels center on the person of Jesus. However, no gospel focuses upon him with the same clarity and force as the Gospel of John. For John the true identity of Jesus is the Eternal Word, sent by the Father to give life to the world. The central importance of faith in Jesus effectively overwhelms every other theme. The Synoptics fill their pages with parables concerning the reign of God, ethical directives, and legal discussions concerning divorce, fasting, and the Sabbath. In John, these issues dissolve within the brilliant light of Jesus' person. John's theology centers on a decision, a choice to believe in Jesus or not. Beginning with the dramatic prologue that presents Jesus as the Word and continuing in almost every encounter with Jesus in the Gospel, this fundamental choice pervades the narration. One must either believe or fail to believe. These two alternatives are the iron rails upon which the story of John's Gospel is grooved to run. The story moves from scene to scene based on the decisions either for or against Jesus.

John does not allow for any middle ground between these two alternatives. There are only two possibilities for human existence. Avoiding the decision to choose between them only leads to disaster. This stark choice is the foundation for a dualism that is a central characteristic of John's Gospel. The world that the evangelist sets before us is divided into two opposing realms corresponding to belief or disbelief in Jesus. The language of the Gospel functions across the paired opposites of light/darkness, life/death, above/below, love/hatred, freedom/slavery, truth/falsehood, God/Satan. To believe in Jesus initiates the believer into the positive realities of these pairs: light, life, what is above, love, freedom, truth, God. To refuse to believe banishes the unbeliever to the opposing realm.

There can be no doubt that this simple choice between two alternatives gives to the Gospel a clarity and a power that can produce great dramatic effects. Much of the impact of key Johannine scenes such as the dialogue with Nicodemus (John 3), the woman at the well (John 4), the man born blind (John 9), and the trial before Pilate (John 18—19) draws its force from the awareness that the response of each character to Jesus is a choice with cosmic consequences. The reader, aware of Jesus' true identity, knows that the stakes are high. He or she can observe from a dramatic distance as the characters in the Gospel seal their fates. This distance permits the author to employ irony and frequent misunderstandings on the part of characters to drive home the revelation of Jesus' true identity to the reader. When all these literary techniques work in coordination, their effect is to produce some of the most moving and artistic passages in the New Testament.

Yet the same dualism that grounds such impressive drama also includes within it a less attractive dimension. The same clear choice that can bestow life and love on one who accepts Jesus can with equal force assign death and hatred to one who refuses to believe. The same dualism that exalts believers to the status of Jesus' friends (John 15:15) and the beloved of God (14:23) can call those who do not believe children of the devil (8:44). In the real world people cannot be so easily separated into good and bad, the loved and the damned. Within the literary world of John's Gospel, however, the choice is starkly simple: Those who do not accept the Johannine Christ have no hope. This definite and unyielding judgment creates an immense potential for anti-Judaism. For, as we shall soon see, the unbelievers whom the Gospel rejects often seem to be the Jewish people.

The History of the Johannine Community

Because the evangelists who composed the gospels in stage three of the tradition have shaped their narration in light of their own situation and history, it is an enormous benefit to the interpreter to know what those historical circumstances were. Unfortunately, there exists little information outside of the gospels themselves by which to ascertain the circumstances of the evangelists' communities. Therefore, scholars have carefully combed through the gospels to extract clues that point to the environment in which each gospel was composed.

The Gospel of John contains several characteristics that are useful in determining its historical setting. This Gospel functions within a Jewish matrix. It must be remembered that being a Christian in the first century of the common era was being a certain kind of Jew. All the early apostles were Jewish. It took some time and a great deal of debate before Gentile believers in Christ began to form an identity apart from Judaism.

There are many sections of John's Gospel that reflect the Jewish origins of the Johannine community. Jesus is presented as a Jew (4:9). He is buried as a Jew (19:40). The Gospel does not shrink from claiming that salvation comes from the Jews (4:22). Jesus participates in many Jewish practices. He attends the great Jewish feasts in Jerusalem. He calls the one God who is worshiped by Jews his Father. He situates himself among the great ancestors of the Jewish people: Abraham, Jacob, and Moses. It would be impossible to understand the rich imagery of the Gospel without familiarity with the Hebrew scriptures. Without such knowledge it would make little sense to identify Jesus with bread (6:35), a shepherd (10:11), a vine (15:1), or living water (4:13–14).

John's Gospel is rooted, then, in Jewish soil. However, we can also find within it signs of turmoil with other Jews. At three key points in the Gospel we are informed that believers in Jesus are in danger of being expelled from the synagogue. The parents of the man born blind refuse to speak because the authorities had agreed to expel from the synagogue anyone who confessed Jesus as the Messiah (9:22). Later we are told that even some of the authorities believed in Jesus but were afraid to confess it lest they be put out of the synagogue (12:42). In Jesus' last discourse he tells his disciples that they can expect to be expelled from the synagogue (16:2). It is unlikely that followers of the historical Jesus were being expelled from synagogues during his ministry or shortly after the resurrection. This exclusion from the synagogue more likely occurred toward the close of the first century, when the exalted claims for Jesus' identity could have spurred fierce debates between the followers of Christ and other Jews. It is likely that such a debate and a resulting exclusion from the synagogue were part of the history of the Johannine community.

How can we explain that positive affirmations of Jewish practices and such significant Jewish opposition are present in the same Gospel? J. L. Martyn, R. E. Brown, and U. C. von Wahlde have drawn on successive editions of the Gospel to explain such tensions. They first identify within the Gospel indications of successive revisions. Then by assigning each revision to a time period and including the witness of the Johannine epistles, they are able to reconstruct a history of the Johannine community. Once the development of the Johannine materials has been identified, differences in expression within the Gospel can be assigned to different periods within the community's history.

In the early years of the Johannine community, when it was close to its Jewish roots, it would be natural for it to express a positive estimation of Judaism. As the community adopted higher and higher claims for the identity and necessity of Christ, it began to experience a growing opposition from its Jewish neighbors. This led eventually to a point in its history at which it was expelled from the synagogue because of its beliefs. This growing estrangement and eventual expulsion from the synagogue were reflected in later editions of the Gospel. The later, more negative evaluations did not, however, totally replace the earlier, more positive beliefs. The resulting Gospel, therefore, includes within it a mix of positive and combative elements, drawn from different periods of the community's history and read back into the ministry of Jesus.

The Opponents of Jesus in the Gospel of John

Within the Gospel, the hostility drawn from the later periods of the community's history becomes linked to John's exclusive dualism. This creates for the Johannine community a powerful engine of rejection of the opponents of Jesus. There is no question about the fate of those who exhibit such opposition. They are quickly relegated to the outer darkness. Therefore, if we are to assess properly the potential for anti-Judaism within the Gospel narration, it will be helpful to examine the specific manner in which the Gospel of John identifies Jewish groups in their opposition to Jesus.

Opposition to Jesus begins early in the Gospel of John. The opening prologue does not take long to assert that "the Word" who came into the world was rejected: "He came to what was his own, and his own people did not accept him" (John 1:11). Within the spiritual dualism of the Gospel, "his own people" refers to all those people who were created by the Word but refuse to believe in him. When viewed through the Jewish matrix of the Gospel, however, the reader can easily conclude a rejection of Jesus' fellow Jews.

After the prologue, the testimony of John the Baptist (1:19) marks the beginning of Jesus' public ministry. During this ministry opposition is presented as coming from certain Jewish groups. This is a picture similar to the one presented in the Synoptic gospels. Yet the Gospel of John refers to fewer opposition groups than do the first three gospels. The Herodians and the Sadducees are not mentioned in John. The scribes and the elders appear only one time each, and this is in the story of the woman caught in the act of adultery (John 7:53—8:11), which most scholars see as a non-Johannine addition to the Gospel. John shares only three terms with the Synoptics by which to describe Jewish opposition groups: the chief priests, the authorities, and the Pharisees. Let us examine each in turn.

> The reference to Jews without any clarification, that is, understood out of context, is a source of confusion and contempt. As we said before, first-century Jewish society was highly divided and cannot be considered as a totality. Jesus had friends as well as critics in the Pharisaic movement, and the Sadducees were somewhat uneasy with his preaching about ritual and sacrifice in the Temple. The social concerns of Jesus were in clear contrast to the Saducean upper-class interests. For that reason, text referring to Jews in the New Testament needs clarification after reading or preaching about it; otherwise, it becomes a pretext for hatred against the Jewish people. Theological anti-Judaism can easily, as it has happened, be transformed into social anti-Semitism.

The term for chief priest *(archiereus)* occurs nineteen times in John. Ten of those occurrences are in the singular, referring to either Caiaphas or Annas. The other nine occurrences identify a religious-leadership group. Consistent with their role in the Synoptics, the chief priests provide significant opposition to Jesus. In the Synoptic gospels their opposition is limited to Jerusalem and the passion. With the exception of the passion predictions that occur during Jesus' ministry, the Synoptics do not mention the chief priests as a force against Jesus until his entry into Jerusalem.

In John the chief priests continue to play a central role during the passion. They send guards to arrest Jesus in the garden (18:3); Pilate identifies them as the agents who hand Jesus over (18:35); they call for Jesus' crucifixion (19:6); they inform Pilate that they have no king but Caesar (19:15); and they demand that Pilate not write that Jesus was the king of the Jews (19:21). Unlike the Synoptic gospels, however, the chief priests in John begin to oppose Jesus even before his triumphal entry into Jerusalem in 12:12. As early as 7:32 the chief priests together with the Pharisees send troops to arrest Jesus, but the effort fails (7:45–46). In 11:45–57 the chief priests together with the Pharisees convene the Sanhedrin and decide to arrest and kill Jesus, and in 12:10 we discover that the chief priests have decided to kill Lazarus as well. As in the Synoptics, the chief priests remain major opponents of Jesus, primarily connected with his death. Their presence in John, however, is more pervasive, plotting Jesus' destruction even before the passion begins.

The second term of religious leadership that John shares with the Synoptics does not describe a specific Jewish sect but rather a general category of people. John speaks of the "authorities" or "rulers" or "leaders" *(hoi archontes)* on seven occasions. Three of these (12:31; 14:30; 16:11) are in the singular and refer to Satan. In 3:1 Nicodemus is described as "a leader of the Jews." The remaining three occurrences are in the plural and seem to refer to those who exercise official authority over the people. In all three cases, however, these authorities seem less opposed to Jesus than do the chief priests or the Pharisees. The three cases occur in 7:26, 7:48, and 12:42. Not without some Johannine irony, in 7:26 some in the crowd ask, "Can it be that the authorities really know that this is the Messiah?" In 7:48 the Pharisees ask the officers who have failed to arrest Jesus, "Has any one of the authorities or of the Pharisees believed in him?" In 12:42 we receive the remarkable answer to that question: "Nevertheless many, even of the authorities, believed in him. But because of the Pharisees they did not confess it, for fear that they would be put out of the synagogue."

The use of "the authorities" in these last three cases, together with the reference to Nicodemus, gives to the term a semipositive thrust in John, when it refers to human agents. The term seems to be used to describe rulers or authorities whose faith is not strong but is nevertheless real. These authorities certainly do not engage in the opposition to Jesus that characterizes the chief priests and Pharisees.

It is important to distinguish the different trends within the Pharisaic movement, which were not specified by the New Testament text that was compiled thirty-five or forty years after the official disappearance of the Pharisaic movement.

The Pharisees considered themselves followers of Ezra, whom they respected and cherished, together with Moses, as founders of Judaism, maintaining the validity of the Oral Law as well as of the Torah (Written Law) as the source of Jewish religiosity and continuity. The Pharisaic movement was a creative and very successful attempt to make biblical law and biblical commandments a daily reality for Jews, implementing at all levels of everyday life the commandments of God. The Pharisees stressed the spiritual meaning of Judaism, in contrast to the Zealots, who were deeply involved in political rebellion; the Pharisaic leadership was willing to submit to foreign domination so long as it did not interfere with the religious life of the community.

The movement of contrast would be the Sadducees, the privileged authority group of the Temple in charge of sacrifice and ritual. While the Sadducees focused on the administration and work of the Temple, indifferent to explanations or commentaries, the Pharisees were eager to make real the experience of God in the home and in daily life.

The main ideas of Pharisaism were the following:

- The belief in a God as an omnipotent, spiritual being, all-wise, all-knowing, all-just, and all-merciful, who established a covenantal relationship with Israel through the keeping of the *Halakhah*. This word has been wrongly translated as law and has created much confusion in the Christian-Jewish relationship. *Halakhah* is not necessarily law but is derived from its basic root *halak* ("to go"); it is a way of being and going as a religious person. The word was wisely created by the rabbinic movement and provides like no other word the perfect description of the Jewish covenantal relationship with God: that is, to implement daily on personal and community levels the call and covenant of God.
- The Pharisees believed in free will and divine retribution, and that the human being was created with two potentials, one for good and one for evil, and the obligation to fortify and exercise the good potential in order to confront and diminish the power of the evil inclination. The human being is responsible for his or her acts.
- Resurrection—The Pharisaic movement believed in the resurrection of the dead.
- Written and Oral Law—The Pharisaic movement maintained that the word of God has been given by the Written Law, the basic commandments as included in the Hebrew Bible, as well as in interpretation, the Oral Law, that expounds the meaning of God's word.
- Worship—The Pharisees believed that God can be worshiped everywhere and that God is present inside and outside the Temple, and that he was not be honored by sacrifices alone. This attitude fostered the synagogue as a place of study and prayer.
- The Pharisees and the New Testament—The Pharisaic movement is believed to have been divided into seven schools or

groups. It is not in vain that Jesus criticizes them seven times, testifying to the existence of those seven schools. The reference to Pharisees as hypocrites, as it appeared in Matthew 23 or in Matthew 3:7 or Luke 18:9–14, was used by the Pharisees themselves. They criticized those who did not set a high ethical standard for themselves and were described as "sore spots" or "plagues of the Pharisaic body" (Mishnah, Tractate *Sotah*—The Suspected Adulteress—3:4).

Was Jesus referring to the whole Pharisaic movement in his criticism or rather to a specific school within the movement? This is important in order to avoid any misunderstanding of Jesus' criticism or using it as a part of the teaching of contempt denigrating and negating the Jewish covenantal relationship.

The Pharisees are the last opposition group that John shares with the Synoptics. With the one exception of Nicodemus, who is a Pharisee nurturing faith in Jesus (3:1–10; 7:50–51; 19:39), John consistently presents the Pharisees as adversaries of Jesus. They question and argue with Jesus (1:24; 8:13; 9:40), cause him to leave Judea (4:1), attack those who are inclined to judge him positively (7:47, 48; 9:13, 15, 16; 12:42), complain that the whole world has gone after Jesus (12:19), and attempt to arrest and kill him (7:32, 45; 11:46, 47, 57). The normal partners of the Pharisees in the Synoptics are the scribes, but this group is missing in John. In the Fourth Gospel the Pharisees act on their own or in conjunction with the chief priests. Together with the chief priests, they plan Jesus' death.

This union between the Pharisees and chief priests is an unusual one for the gospels, occurring only two times outside of John (Matt 21:45; 27:62). Moreover, the linking of the Pharisees and chief priest raises historical questions. In John 11:47 the Pharisees are said to convoke the Sanhedrin together with the chief priests. The three groups usually associated with the Sanhedrin are the chief priests, the elders, and the scribes. This is attested by the Synoptics and seems historically accurate. Why then are the Pharisees connected to the chief priests and the Sanhedrin in John? It is helpful in answering this question to recognize that John has a tendency of inserting the Pharisees as replacements for other opposition groups. For example, Matthew (26:3–4) asserts that the chief priests and elders conspire with Caiaphas to arrest and kill Jesus. John (11:47–53) replaces the elders with the Pharisees. In Mark (14:43), the crowd that comes to arrest Jesus is sent by the chief priests, the scribes, and the elders. In John (18:3), the soldiers who come to arrest Jesus are sent by the chief priests and the Pharisees.

What is going on here? John's inclination to insert the Pharisees into the narrative and their unlikely linkage with the chief priests indicate that John is reading some of the history of his own community back into the events of Jesus' ministry and death. With their increasing prominence after the destruction of the Temple in 70 CE, the Pharisees became the chief opponents of the Johannine community. This explains why the evangelist is more interested in them than in the other Jewish groups that had come down to him in the tradition. The chief priests were too central in the tradition to be dislodged. The elders and the scribes, however, were less established. This made it easier for John to replace them with the Pharisees, who had much more relevance to his own community. In other words, the mention of the Pharisees in connection to Jesus' arrest in the garden (18:3) and their linkage with the chief priests in convening the Sanhedrin (11:47) reflect their prominence at the end of the first century. We should not, therefore, assume that the presence of the Pharisees in these scenes is an indication of the powers they may have possessed or associations they may have held before the destruction of the Temple.

Hoi Ioudaioi in the Gospel of John

The most problematic term that John uses to describe a Jewish group within the Gospel is the Greek phrase *hoi Ioudaioi*. This phrase is usually translated "the Jews." However, as will soon become clear, a significant debate continues over the appropriateness of that translation. Within the four gospels the word occurs eighty-seven times. Of those occurrences seventy-one are present in John. It is clear, then, that the term has special meaning in John's Gospel. It will take us some time to outline what that meaning could be.

It is useful to distinguish between a neutral and a polemical use of *hoi Ioudaioi*. In the neutral use a group of people are being presented as a distinct religious or cultural entity without any negative evaluation. Thus the Gospel mentions "Jewish rites of purification" (2:6), "a festival of the Jews" (5:1), "Nicodemus, a leader of the Jews" (3:1), or the Samaritan woman's comment to Jesus, "How is it that you, a Jew, ask a drink of me?" (4:9). The neutral use also identifies groups that betray no hostility to Jesus or his disciples, such as the Jews who believed in Jesus (11:45) and those who read the inscription on the cross (19:20). The phrase "the King of the Jews" occurs six times in John and should be included in the neutral sense.

The Greek phrase *hoi Ioudaioi* is generally translated as "the Jews." It appears frequently in John and requires some clarification. It is important to state that the expression might refer to those members of the Jewish community who did not believe in Jesus and who opposed him. Taken in a general way, and out of context, it is the source of the deicide accusation, the accusation that brought so much pain through the centuries and is ever-present in passion plays like the Oberammergau Passion Play in Germany. A short explanation would help the listener understand that the term does not cover the whole Jewish community, but perhaps refers to a specific group that was in opposition to Jesus' message.

The second way in which *hoi Ioudaioi* can be used in John's Gospel is the polemical sense. It occurs in at least thirty-one of the seventy-one instances of *hoi Ioudaioi* within the Gospel. The polemical use is characterized by hostility toward Jesus. Those who are described in this sense try to slander, attack, and kill him. Sometimes the stance is lessened to only skepticism or disagreement. But those who are described by the polemical usage are clearly Jesus' opponents. They are never portrayed in a positive light.

Moreover, within the text of John the polemical sense can suddenly emerge as a replacement for another more traditional Jewish group. The Pharisees can find themselves abruptly dismissed from a particular story and replaced by *hoi Ioudaioi* (8:22; 9:18). This same unexpected exchange occurs with the crowd in 6:41. Throughout the passion narrative, roles that within the Synoptic gospels are played by the chief priests, elders, and scribes are filled in John by *hoi Ioudaioi*. They are the ones who send their police to arrest Jesus (18:12), who call for his death (19:7, 12, 14), and to whom Jesus says he will be handed over (18:36).

Therefore, in scenes throughout the Gospel when there is opposition to Jesus, the evangelist shows a remarkable freedom to insert *hoi Ioudaioi* as a replacement for opposition groups that are described with much more specificity in the Synoptics and even in other places in John's own Gospel.

We have already noted how the Pharisees in John can displace other Jewish groups. Now we see *hoi Ioudaioi* following a similar pattern. Again, this tendency can be connected to the history of the Johannine community. When the Johannine community began to experience opposition resulting from its increasing elevation of the identity of Jesus, that opposition likely came from Pharisaic sources. In revising its gospel traditions, the community felt free to replace the more traditional opposition to Jesus (the elders and the scribes) with its own opponents, the Pharisees. Still later in the history of the community, when its beliefs had occasioned expulsion from the synagogue, the evangelist chose to replace Jewish groups including the Pharisees with *hoi Ioudaioi*. The imprecision and anachronistic quality of this term did not seem to bother the evangelist, writing in a period in which the bonds with Jews outside his community had been severed. Overall, then, the use of more generalized terms to identify the opponents of Jesus within the Gospel follows the historical stages of the Johannine community, which developed from its Jewish beginnings to an eventual separation from the synagogue.

To What Group Does *hoi Ioudaioi* Refer?

No doubt, the observant reader already has noticed my reluctance to translate *hoi Ioudaioi* into English. This results from an ongoing debate within the scholarly community as to what the correct translation should be. The complex manner in which we have seen this term read back into the Gospel creates a barrage of problems in ascertaining its proper meaning. Because the polemical use of the term aligns it with the negative side of John's dualism, this debate over translation is played for very high stakes. The Gospel clearly uses *hoi Ioudaioi* to identify those who do not believe in Jesus and who actively oppose him. They are therefore in John the premier example of those who are opposed to God. Who, then, are those to whom the evangelist assigns such a fateful role?

On one level the answer to this question is simple. They are the Jews who refused to accept the Johannine community's belief in Jesus and who expelled John's community from the synagogue. As we have seen, it was most likely this later experience of rejection that motivated the Gospel writer to employ this term. But it will not do to translate *hoi Ioudaioi* in this light. Only confusion would result from a verse that reads: "Then Jesus spoke to those Jews who expelled the

Johannine community from the synagogue around 90 CE." In translations, historical horizons must be respected. Since the term has been read back into a narration presenting events that are taking place at the beginning of the first century, the translator must decide what characters it describes within the time period of the story.

It is on the level of the Gospel story that the problems of understanding *hoi Ioudaioi* become most complex. For, as we have already seen, the term in its polemical sense will suddenly emerge as a replacement for another term. Then, at times, it will quickly recede again. Thus the translator will need to determine the group to which the term refers chiefly by context. Thankfully, one referent of the term is very difficult to maintain—that *hoi Ioudaioi* is meant to refer to all Jewish people. In most of the polemical occurrences a translation indicating "all the Jews" or "the whole Jewish nation" does not fit the story. For example, the Gospel tells us that a man who was cured reports to "the Jews" (5:16). Later, we are informed that the parents of the man born blind and the disciples after the resurrection both stand in "fear of the Jews" (9:22; 20:19). Yet it is clear that the man who was cured, the parents of the man born blind, and the disciples are all Jewish themselves. Therefore, *hoi Ioudaioi* in these verses must refer to some subset of Jews within the story.

What subset could this be? One opinion would hold that *hoi Ioudaioi* should be translated "the Judeans." In the ancient world *hoi Ioudaioi* was regularly used to refer to all Jews (as distinct from Samaritans, Romans, or Greeks). But *hoi Ioudaioi* could also be used to refer only to those Jews who were connected to the tribe of Judah. One can argue, therefore, that *hoi Ioudaioi* in the Gospel of John does not refer to all Jews but only to those who live in the land of Judah. In this view, our translations would consistently speak of "the Judeans" rather than "the Jews."

This argument works well in certain verses of the Gospel. For example, it makes sense for the narrator to say that Jesus did not wish to go to Judea "because the *Judeans* were looking for an opportunity to kill him" (7:1). Likewise when Jesus announces that he wishes to go again to Judea, the translation is actually clearer if the disciples say, "Rabbi, the *Judeans* were just now going to stone you, and are you going there again?" (11:8). When, however, this translation is attempted for other occurrences of *hoi Ioudaioi* within the Gospel, we end up with some rather strange expressions, such as "the Passover of the Judeans" (2:13) and "the king of the Judeans" (19:19). Therefore, although "the Judeans" serves as a fitting translation of *hoi Ioudaioi* at several points within the Gospel, in most of the polemical usages it is difficult to find a reason why the Gospel would be singling out this particular subgroup of Jews as the enemies of Jesus.

A more promising referent for *hoi Ioudaioi* is "the Jewish Temple leadership." We have already seen how *hoi Ioudaioi* can suddenly replace the Pharisees and other religious groups. In many of the polemical usages of *hoi Ioudaioi*, those to whom it refers do things that the Temple authorities do: sending priests and Levites on a mission (1:19), sending police for an arrest (18:12), negotiating with Pilate (19:31). Judging from these contexts, "the Temple leadership" emerges as the term's true referent.

Yet there remain a number of occurrences in which this referent is inappropriate. For example, in chapter six of the Gospel (verses 41 and 52), Jesus is arguing with "the crowd" and suddenly is said to be arguing with *hoi Ioudaioi*. Here it seems that the term is functioning as a substitute for "the crowd" or better "some in the crowd."

The problem of how to understand and translate *hoi Ioudaioi* does not, therefore, lend itself to a simple solution. Although it can refer to all the Jewish people, in John's Gospel it does not seem to carry that connotation when used polemically. In most contexts the Temple authorities serve as the Jewish subgroup to which the phrase refers. Yet even that approach must allow for exceptions. It seems best, therefore, to examine each occurrence and translate it according to its proximate associations and context.

The complexity of translating the polemical usage of *hoi Ioudaioi* arises from the influence that later historical events have imposed on the Gospel. The opposition experienced by the Johannine community at the end of the first century has inclined the evangelist to insert *hoi Ioudaioi* into his narrative when Jesus faces opposition from the Pharisees, chief priests, or crowds.

Pastoral Sensitivity in the Use of *hoi Ioudaioi*

Since the polemical use of *hoi Ioudaioi* is always aligned with the negative side of John's exclusive dualism, understanding the significance of the term is of extreme importance. When a polemical usage is translated "the Jews," there is no distinction present in the translation that separates it from the neutral usages. Therefore, a reader can easily draw the conclusion that it was the entire Jewish people who were always opposed to Jesus and constantly seeking his death. The Vatican Commission for Religious Relations with the Jews recognized this problem when it issued "Guidelines and Suggestions for Implementing the Conciliar Declaration, *Nostrae Aetate* (n. 4)" in 1975. In guiding the translators of liturgical texts, the commission encouraged the use of biblical studies to bring out the explicit meaning of the original languages. It used the example of *hoi Ioudaioi,* stating that in John's Gospel it "sometimes according to context means 'the leaders of the Jews,' or 'the adversaries of Jesus,' terms which express better the thought of the Evangelist and avoid appearing to arraign the Jewish people as such."

The preacher and catechist should be aware of the complexity of this term within John's Gospel and find ways to remind those they serve of the danger of applying it to the whole Jewish people. A careful reading of the Gospel itself will demonstrate that not all Jews were opposed to Jesus. However, false perceptions of the relationship between Jesus and the Jewish people persist. One can still find Christians who believe that the Jewish people as a whole were responsible for Jesus' death and that they have been therefore rejected by God. To allow our congregations to understand *hoi Ioudaioi* as simply "the Jews" would support such dangerous errors, giving the impression that these beliefs could be supported on scriptural or historical grounds.

John's Retrograding Tendency

Throughout our discussion of Jesus' opponents in John, it has already become clear that the conflicts that the Johannine community experienced have been read back into the Gospel. John enhances this retrograding tendency by reading back into earlier scenes of Jesus' ministry some of the actions that were taken against Jesus at his arrest, trial, and execution.

John's Gospel is heavily shaped by theological convictions. The saving significance of Jesus' death can be found throughout the narrative. John's concern to present the cross as the chosen means of Jesus' glorification overrides any desire for sequential development or empirical history. Therefore, throughout his account of Jesus' ministry, John scatters many references to the constant desire to kill Jesus (5:18; 7:1, 25; 8:37, 40, 59; 10:31; 11:8, 50). It seems to be simply a given in John's narrative that there is a plot to destroy Jesus. This should not lead us to conclude that there was such a scheme from the opening days of Jesus' historical ministry. Rather, it is more likely that John, writing from a theological-spiritual perspective, sees the opposition to Jesus in terms of a dualistic and cosmic constant. If there is light, there is darkness. If there is faith, there is unbelief. If there are those who love Jesus, there are those who seek to kill him.

John expands the pervasive opposition to Jesus by moving forward in the narrative the official decision to kill him. Within their passion narratives both Mark (14:53–65) and Matthew (26:57–68) present a night trial before the Sanhedrin resulting in the verdict of death. Luke (22:66–71) presents the meeting of the Sanhedrin in the morning resulting in the decision to hand Jesus over to Pilate. John has no meeting of the Sanhedrin during his passion narrative. There is only an inquiry before Annas in which we hear none of the Synoptic charges and are given no verdict (18:19–24). In John the official decision to sentence Jesus to death occurs before Passover. An official Sanhedrin meeting is called by the chief priests and Pharisees several weeks before Passover in response to Jesus' raising of Lazarus (11:45–53). Thus, in John, Jesus is not condemned by the Sanhedrin after his arrest but before his entry into Jerusalem.

Moreover, the questions and charges that are part of the session before the Sanhedrin in the Synoptics also seem to have been moved forward by John into the debates that Jesus has with his opponents during his ministry. For example, the question of Jesus' identity as "the Messiah, Son of the Blessed One" found in all the Synoptic sessions before the Sanhedrin (Mark 14:62; Matt 26:63–64; Luke 22:67) is very similar to the matter debated by Jesus and his opponents on the feast of the Dedication (John 10:24–25, 33, 36). As a result of this, in John's Gospel the interrogation of Jesus by those who seek to kill him is not limited to a single scene during the passion. It is scattered throughout the ministry (primarily chapters 5 to 12) as Jesus debates with his opponents.

The bitter controversies that the Johannine community fought with its opponents not only color the narration of the Gospel in the final days of Jesus' life but shape the christological debates between Jesus and his opponents throughout the entire Gospel. Indeed, if we accept the charge of rejection found in the prologue (1:11) as an indication of the opposition that is to follow, the polemic between Jesus and those who will not believe begins even before the public ministry. We must be careful not to conclude that these early plots against Jesus in John's narrative accurately reflect an opposition that was leveled against the historical Jesus.

Lectionary Commentary

The commentary that follows will apply the issues treated in the Introduction to specific passages of John's Gospel that are part of the Roman Catholic lectionary. My aim is to assist the preacher and catechist in recognizing passages that pertain to issues of Jewish-Christian relations. Lectionary selections that carry no obvious reference to Jewish-Christian issues will not be treated. The passages to be examined have been drawn from those assigned to Sundays and major feasts.

By highlighting ideas and statements within the passages that display the positive relationship between Jesus and Judaism, the commentary will provide opportunities for the preacher and catechist to communicate a more healthy and accurate understanding of Judaism as the parent of the Christian faith tradition. Negative and prejudicial views against Jews and Judaism that could be derived from the lectionary selections will also be discussed. In this way the pastoral minister will be alerted to the potential for harm within the scriptures and be encouraged to oppose it.

As a pastor myself, I am well aware that the homily is not the place to engage in prolonged adult education or to present scripture study on the historical-critical methods. Moreover, the anti-Jewish potential that can be found within the gospels is not the good news we are charged to proclaim. However, in the proclamation of the message of salvation, which is our duty and privilege to set before God's people, a homilist should certainly be aware of harmful misunderstandings of the biblical text and preach in such a way as to defuse them. The notes that follow are intended to assist in such an effort.

Readings from the Gospel
of John in Cycle A

1
Christmas, Mass during the Day, Cycles A, B, C • John 1:1–18

1:1 In the beginning was the Word,
and the Word was with God,
and the Word was God.
2 He was in the beginning with God.
3 All things came to be through him,
and without him nothing came to be.
What came to be 4 through him was life,
and this life was the light of the human race;
5 the light shines in the darkness,
and the darkness has not overcome it.
6 A man named John was sent from God.
7 He came for testimony, to testify to the light,
so that all might believe through him.
8 He was not the light,
but came to testify to the light.
9 The true light, which enlightens everyone, was coming into the world.
10 He was in the world,
and the world came to be through him,
but the world did not know him.
11 He came to what was his own,
but his own people did not accept him.
12 But to those who did accept him
he gave power to become children of God,
to those who believe in his name,
13 who were born not by natural generation
nor by human choice nor by a man's decision
but of God.
14 And the Word became flesh
and made his dwelling among us,
and we saw his glory,
the glory as of the Father's only Son,
full of grace and truth.

¹⁵ John testified to him and cried out, saying,
  "This was he of whom I said,
  'The one who is coming after me ranks ahead of me
  because he existed before me.'"
¹⁶ From his fullness we have all received,
  grace in place of grace,
  ¹⁷ because while the law was given through Moses,
  grace and truth came through Jesus Christ.
¹⁸ No one has ever seen God.
The only Son, God, who is at the Father's side,
  has revealed him.*

In all three cycles of the Catholic lectionary, the first eighteen verses of John's Gospel are assigned for Masses during the day on Christmas, as well as on the Second Sunday after Christmas. These verses comprise the prologue of the Gospel. Their vocabulary and style indicate origins in a liturgical hymn, most likely developed within the Johannine community. It is possible that the prologue was appended to the Gospel as a later addition, serving as an introduction to the narrative of Jesus' earthly ministry. With artful force it presents "the Word" *(logos)* to the reader, drawing the inescapable conclusion that the words and deeds of Jesus to follow are indeed those of the Word who was with God from the beginning of creation. The obvious connection to Christmas is verse 14, in which we are told that the Word became flesh and lived among us. The prologue is rich with insights for preaching and teaching. The potential for anti-Jewish bias is present in only a muted and ambiguous way, chiefly in verses 11, 16, and 17.

In 1:11 we are told that the Word who came into the world came to "his own." The Greek word for "his own" is an adjectival form used here with the article as a substantive. It is used twice in this verse, first in the neuter form and then in the masculine. Neither time is it specified to what reality the term refers. Because the first use is neuter, it seems to refer to nonpersonal possessions belonging to the Word—*what* is the Word's own. In contrast, the masculine form seems to refer to persons—*who* are the Word's own. The challenge, then, is to determine what are the realities and who are the persons to which "his own" refers.

---

*While the scriptural excerpts taken from the *Lectionary for Mass for use in the Dioceses of the United States of America* are from the New American Bible, other scriptural excerpts, in the general text and in the rabbinic notes and commentaries, are from the New Revised Standard Version: Catholic Edition.

Many commentators read the neuter form as referring to the Jewish heritage or territory and the masculine form to the Jewish people. In this interpretation, the Word became a part of the Jewish people and they rejected him. Other commentators, however, argue that the adjectival forms should ñot be limited to Jews but rather extend to the entire world and all the people in it. This universal approach is strengthened when the two uses of "his own" in verse 11 are associated with earlier verses in the prologue. The neuter form can be seen to parallel "all things" of the world that came to be through the Word (1:3), and the masculine form may well refer back to "the human race" for which the Word was the light (1:4). Read in this way, verse 11 claims that the Word came into "his own" world which was created through him, yet he was rejected by some of "his own" creatures whom he sought to enlighten.

Since the precise referent for the two adjectives is debated, a more cautious translation would leave the adjectives unspecified: "to his own he came, yet his own did not accept him" (as in the 1970 edition of the New American Bible). To translate the masculine form as "his own people did not accept him" (as in the lectionary translation) will cause most readers to understand a reference to the Jewish people. By such a translation what is unspecified in the text is clarified in a way that carries anti-Jewish potential. A more literal translation recognizes the ambiguity of the text and reduces the probability of detrimental interpretations.

Preachers and catechists who focus on this verse should be aware of the choices made in translation and the underlying ambiguity of the terms. However one chooses to interpret "his own," the minister should strive to proclaim the good news of the incarnation without making Jewish rejection its backdrop. That some do not believe is indeed an aspect of John's dualism. That the majority of Jews did not choose to accept Christ as Messiah is a fact of history. Christmas, however, is not the time to emphasize the failure of belief, but rather its gracious beginnings. If for some reason the preacher or catechist will insist on analyzing a lack of faith, let the exposition focus upon the inadequacies in ourselves rather than the failures we may perceive in our Jewish brothers and sisters.

The other verses of the prologue that carry anti-Jewish potential are 1:16–17. Here a contrast is drawn between two types of grace (verse 16) together with a similar contrast between the Law that was given by Moses and the grace and truth that have come through Jesus Christ (verse 17). In 1:16 the Greek preposition *anti* makes its only appearance in the Johannine writings, linking the two occurrences of "grace." How should it be translated? *Anti* can carry the sense of replacement or of temporal order. If replacement is chosen, it will translate as "grace in place of grace" (as in the lectionary translation). Here the idea is that one grace (the incarnation) replaces another (God's love for Israel). If the sense of temporal order is adopted, it will translate as "grace upon grace" (as in the New Revised Standard Version) or "love following upon love" (as in the 1970 edition of the New American Bible). This translation implies that the grace of the incarnation builds upon the grace of God's love for Israel. Grace is not being replaced but is accumulating.

The choice for temporal order can be strengthened by recognizing a parallel between verse 16 and the following verse. Verse 17 links the Law given by Moses to the grace and truth of Christ. The reference to Moses is helpful. Several times within the Gospel John treats Moses with high regard. Philip tells Nathanael that Jesus is the one about whom Moses wrote (1:45), and later in the Gospel Jesus agrees with the insight (5:46). Jesus uses the example of Moses lifting up the serpent in the desert as a reference to his own glorification (3:14). Jesus even uses Moses to assist in a debate with his opponents, claiming that although Moses gave the Law, they do not obey it (7:19). Since John values the role of Moses, it gives strength to the opinion that verses 16 and 17 should be read as accumulation rather than replacement. Both verses would then pull in the same direction, presenting the grace of Christ as building upon the previous grace of God to Israel.

This approach of accumulation provides an attractive possibility in proclaiming the Christmas message. It is clear to all that the good news of this feast is the remarkable gift of the Word, God's only begotten Son, becoming one of us. The preacher or catechist might reflect on how consistently gracious our God is. Although the incarnation and redemption were the climax of God's gift, they were not anomalies. God's history with us has been all grace from creation forward. God continues to bless and guide us today in our families, jobs, and aspirations. As the preacher or catechist presents this consistent sweep of God's love, it would be appropriate and healing to highlight the call of Israel as an integral expression of God's grace and truth. It would also be fitting to remind those who come to celebrate Christ's birth that the promises of God to Israel and God's love for the Jewish people continue to this day.

2
Second Sunday after Christmas, Cycles A, B, C • John 1:1–18

See Christmas, Mass during the Day, above.

3

Holy Thursday, Mass of the Lord's Supper, Cycles A, B, C • John 13:1–15

¹³:¹ Before the feast of Passover, Jesus knew that his hour had come
to pass from this world to the Father.

He loved his own in the world and he loved them to the end.

² The devil had already induced Judas, son of Simon the Iscariot, to hand
him over.

So, during supper,

³ fully aware that the Father had put everything into his power
and that he had come from God and was returning to God,

⁴ he rose from supper and took off his outer garments.

He took a towel and tied it around his waist.

⁵ Then he poured water into a basin
and began to wash the disciples' feet
and dry them with the towel around his waist.

⁶ He came to Simon Peter, who said to him,

"Master, are you going to wash my feet?"

⁷ Jesus answered and said to him,

"What I am doing, you do not understand now,
but you will understand later."

⁸ Peter said to him, "You will never wash my feet."

Jesus answered him,

"Unless I wash you, you will have no inheritance with me."

⁹ Simon Peter said to him,

"Master, then not only my feet, but my hands and head as well."

¹⁰ Jesus said to him,

"Whoever has bathed has no need except to have his feet washed,
for he is clean all over;
so you are clean, but not all."

¹¹ For he knew who would betray him;
for this reason, he said, "Not all of you are clean."

¹² So when he had washed their feet
and put his garments back on and reclined at table again,

he said to them, "Do you realize what I have done for you?
[13] You call me 'teacher' and 'master,' and rightly so, for indeed I am.
[14] If I, therefore, the master and teacher, have washed your feet,
    you ought to wash one another's feet.
[15] I have given you a model to follow,
    so that as I have done for you, you should also do."

The foot washing from John's Gospel is read at the evening Mass of the Lord's Supper in all three cycles. This passage is relatively free from any anti-Jewish potential. It also provides a positive connection between the Christian faith and the Jewish tradition. The emphasis in preaching on this reading is usually placed on the role of love and service. This flows from the explanation that Jesus gives of his action in verses 14–15. There he tells the disciples to follow his example.

It is sometimes overlooked, however, that another explanation of the foot washing is given in verses 7–8. There Jesus insists to Peter that "unless I wash you, you will have no inheritance with me." What is the significance of this "washing," and why does Jesus see it as essential? It is best to understand the washing of Peter as a sign of his participation in the passion-glorification of Jesus and the saving effects that will flow from it. In other words, these verses insist that a true disciple of Jesus must be one who embraces the saving reality of the cross. From this perspective the meaning of the foot washing is expanded beyond that of mutual service and becomes a way to share in the salvation of Christ. The first verse of this passage confirms this interpretation. There the evangelist tells us that the supper took place before the festival of the Passover when Jesus knew "his hour" had come. Jesus' "hour" is John's way of naming Jesus' return to the Father through his death and glorification. The foot washing is a means to share in Jesus' hour. John has carefully associated it with the feast of Passover.

Throughout the Gospel John uses various Jewish feasts to identify different sections of the narration. Unlike the Synoptic gospels, which relate only one journey of Jesus to Jerusalem at the end of his ministry, John recounts several visits of Jesus to Jerusalem, usually connected with the celebration of Jewish festivals. Chapter five is associated with the Sabbath. In chapter six we are told that the multiplication of loaves took place near the feast of Passover (6:4). Chapters seven through nine are associated with the feast of

Tabernacles (7:2, 14, 37). In chapter ten Jesus is in the Temple area while the feast of the Dedication was taking place (10:22). As Jesus' return to the Father approaches, the evangelist tips his hand that Jesus' hour will be associated with the feast of Passover (11:55; 12:1). The first verse in this lectionary selection reminds us that Passover is now imminent.

John continues to link the death and resurrection of Jesus to Passover in the passion narrative itself. There, Jesus' condemnation to death corresponds to the time when the Temple priests began to slaughter the lambs for the feast (19:14). For John, Jesus' sacrifice is our new Passover. Jesus' words to Peter at the foot washing are a reference to that saving activity.

It is possible, of course, to speak of Christ's Passover in such a way as to replace and denigrate the Jewish feast. The sensitive preacher and catechist will avoid this. Rather than speaking of replacement of Passover, the preacher can use its presence in this text to emphasize continuity. We believe that Christ is our Passover, our way to freedom and salvation. We also believe that it is the same saving God who freed Israel from the slavery of Egypt. It was Jesus, the Jew, believing in God's love through the Passover of his people, who laid down his life in love for us.

Rabbinic Notes on the Foot Washing at the Last Supper: John 13:1–15

This passage highlights the important notions of "clean" and "unclean" in Jewish life. Here, it would appear that Jesus is speaking metaphorically to describe the inner life of Judas Iscariot as "unclean" by his imminent betrayal. But what does Jewish law mean by the notion of "unclean," so central to John's description here of the Last Supper? The concept is best found in Leviticus 11—17 and Numbers 19, describing a condition in which a person or object cannot have contact with the Temple or its cult. Here, Jesus is accommodating a text from Mishnah, *Kelim,* 1,5—"[T]here are ten grades of uncleanness that emanate from man—one whose atonement is [yet] incomplete is prohibited [to consume of] holy sacrifices, but is permitted to [eat of the] priest's due and tithe; one that had immersed himself in the ritual bath, the selfsame day [but sundown has not yet arrived] is forbidden to eat of [holy sacrifices and] priest's due, but is permitted [to eat of] tithes"—to his own sacrificial adaptation of the Passover meal as found in John. By washing the feet of his own disciples, Jesus provides them with an example of how to gain inner purity in preparation for participation in his sacrificial self-giving. Such a ritual condition could be most often corrected by ablutions—such as those done by Jesus in this scene from the Gospel. Indeed, in this story, John has Jesus apply the notion of impurity to his own disciples and their lack of readiness to participate in his unique Passover meal. Iscariot is singled out by Jesus as "unclean," that is, as someone who refuses this important state of inner and outer readiness to accept God's will. Frequently, the name of "Judas" has been used in an anti-Jewish way, most notably as a synonym for "traitor" in English. It should be remembered, however, that the personal failure of Judas to be loyal to his friendship with Christ—producing this special notion of "impurity" in the teaching of Jesus just prior to his own sacrifice of self for the world—can never be used as a generalization for all Jews or for Judaism as a religion. The danger of possible anti-Judaism in this text arises, in short, from an occasional Christian tendency to read into it an anger against the "unclean" Judas, somehow typical of all Jews as allegedly responsible for the death of Jesus.

4
Good Friday, Cycles A, B, C
John 18:1—19:42

^{18:1}Jesus went out with his disciples across the Kidron valley
 to where there was a garden,
 into which he and his disciples entered.
²Judas his betrayer also knew the place,
 because Jesus had often met there with his disciples.
³So Judas got a band of soldiers and guards
 from the chief priests and the Pharisees
 and went there with lanterns, torches, and weapons.
⁴Jesus, knowing everything that was going to happen to him,
 went out and said to them, "Whom are you looking for?"
⁵They answered him, "Jesus the Nazorean."
He said to them, "I AM."
Judas his betrayer was also with them.
⁶When he said to them, "I AM, "
 they turned away and fell to the ground.
⁷So he again asked them,
 "Whom are you looking for?"
They said, "Jesus the Nazorean."
⁸Jesus answered,
 "I told you that I AM.
So if you are looking for me, let these men go."
⁹This was to fulfill what he had said,
 "I have not lost any of those you gave me."
¹⁰Then Simon Peter, who had a sword, drew it,
 struck the high priest's slave, and cut off his right ear.
The slave's name was Malchus.
¹¹Jesus said to Peter,
 "Put your sword into its scabbard.
Shall I not drink the cup that the Father gave me?"

¹²So the band of soldiers, the tribune, and the Jewish guards seized Jesus,
 bound him, ¹³and brought him to Annas first.

He was the father-in-law of Caiaphas,
    who was high priest that year.
[14]It was Caiaphas who had counseled the Jews
    that it was better that one man should die rather than the people.

[15]Simon Peter and another disciple followed Jesus.
Now the other disciple was known to the high priest,
    and he entered the courtyard of the high priest with Jesus.
[16]But Peter stood at the gate outside.
So the other disciple, the acquaintance of the high priest,
    went out and spoke to the gatekeeper and brought Peter in.
[17]Then the maid who was the gatekeeper said to Peter,
    "You are not one of this man's disciples, are you?"
He said, "I am not."
[18]Now the slaves and the guards were standing around a charcoal fire
    that they had made, because it was cold,
    and were warming themselves.
Peter was also standing there keeping warm.

[19]The high priest questioned Jesus
    about his disciples and about his doctrine.
[20]Jesus answered him,
    "I have spoken publicly to the world.
I have always taught in a synagogue
    or in the temple area where all the Jews gather,
    and in secret I have said nothing. [21]Why ask me?
Ask those who heard me what I said to them.
They know what I said."
[22]When he had said this,
    one of the temple guards standing there struck Jesus and said,
    "Is this the way you answer the high priest?"
[23]Jesus answered him,
    "If I have spoken wrongly, testify to the wrong;
    but if I have spoken rightly, why do you strike me?"
[24]Then Annas sent him bound to Caiaphas the high priest.

[25]Now Simon Peter was standing there keeping warm.
And they said to him,
    "You are not one of his disciples, are you?"
He denied it and said,
    "I am not."
[26]One of the slaves of the high priest,
    a relative of the one whose ear Peter had cut off, said,
    "Didn't I see you in the garden with him?"

[27]Again Peter denied it.
And immediately the cock crowed.

[28]Then they brought Jesus from Caiaphas to the praetorium.
It was morning.
And they themselves did not enter the praetorium,
   in order not to be defiled so that they could eat the Passover.
[29]So Pilate came out to them and said,
   "What charge do you bring against this man?"
[30]They answered and said to him,
   "If he were not a criminal,
   we would not have handed him over to you."
[31]At this, Pilate said to them,
   "Take him yourselves, and judge him according to your law."
The Jews answered him,
   "We do not have the right to execute anyone,"
   [32]in order that the word of Jesus might be fulfilled
   that he said indicating the kind of death he would die.
[33]So Pilate went back into the praetorium
   and summoned Jesus and said to him,
   "Are you the King of the Jews?"
[34]Jesus answered,
   "Do you say this on your own
   or have others told you about me?"
[35]Pilate answered,
   "I am not a Jew, am I?
Your own nation and the chief priests handed you over to me.
What have you done?"
[36]Jesus answered,
   "My kingdom does not belong to this world.
If my kingdom did belong to this world,
   my attendants would be fighting
   to keep me from being handed over to the Jews.
But as it is, my kingdom is not here."
[37]So Pilate said to him,
   "Then you are a king?"
Jesus answered,
   "You say I am a king.
For this I was born and for this I came into the world,
   to testify to the truth.
Everyone who belongs to the truth listens to my voice."
[38]Pilate said to him, "What is truth?"

When he had said this,
>he again went out to the Jews and said to them,
>"I find no guilt in him.
³⁹But you have a custom that I release one prisoner to you at Passover.
Do you want me to release to you the King of the Jews?"
⁴⁰They cried out again,
>"Not this one but Barabbas!"
Now Barabbas was a revolutionary.

¹⁹:¹Then Pilate took Jesus and had him scourged.
²And the soldiers wove a crown out of thorns and placed it on his head,
>and clothed him in a purple cloak,
>>³and they came to him and said,
>>"Hail, King of the Jews!"
And they struck him repeatedly.
⁴Once more Pilate went out and said to them,
>"Look, I am bringing him out to you,
>so that you may know that I find no guilt in him."
⁵So Jesus came out,
>wearing the crown of thorns and the purple cloak.
⁶And he said to them, "Behold, the man!"
When the chief priests and the guards saw him they cried out,
>"Crucify him, crucify him!"
Pilate said to them,
>"Take him yourselves and crucify him.
I find no guilt in him."
⁷The Jews answered,
>"We have a law, and according to that law he ought to die,
>because he made himself the Son of God."
⁸Now when Pilate heard this statement,
>he became even more afraid,
>>⁹and went back into the praetorium and said to Jesus,
>>"Where are you from?"
Jesus did not answer him.
¹⁰So Pilate said to him,
>"Do you not speak to me?
Do you not know that I have power to release you
>and I have power to crucify you?"
¹¹Jesus answered him,
>"You would have no power over me
>if it had not been given to you from above.
For this reason the one who handed me over to you
>has the greater sin."

[12]Consequently, Pilate tried to release him; but the Jews cried out,
   "If you release him, you are not a Friend of Caesar.
Everyone who makes himself a king opposes Caesar."

[13]When Pilate heard these words he brought Jesus out
   and seated him on the judge's bench
   in the place called Stone Pavement, in Hebrew, Gabbatha.
[14]It was preparation day for Passover, and it was about noon.
And he said to the Jews,
   "Behold, your king!"
[15]They cried out,
   "Take him away, take him away!   Crucify him!"
Pilate said to them,
   "Shall I crucify your king?"
The chief priests answered,
   "We have no king but Caesar."
[16]Then he handed him over to them to be crucified.

So they took Jesus, [17]and, carrying the cross himself,
   he went out to what is called the Place of the Skull,
   in Hebrew, Golgotha.
[18]There they crucified him, and with him two others,
   one on either side, with Jesus in the middle.
[19]Pilate also had an inscription written and put on the cross.
It read,
   "Jesus the Nazorean, the King of the Jews."
[20]Now many of the Jews read this inscription,
   because the place where Jesus was crucified was near the city;
   and it was written in Hebrew, Latin, and Greek.
[21]So the chief priests of the Jews said to Pilate,
   "Do not write 'The King of the Jews,'
   but that he said, 'I am the King of the Jews'."
[22]Pilate answered,
   "What I have written, I have written."

[23]When the soldiers had crucified Jesus,
   they took his clothes and divided them into four shares,
   a share for each soldier.
They also took his tunic, but the tunic was seamless,
   woven in one piece from the top down.
[24]So they said to one another,
   "Let's not tear it, but cast lots for it to see whose it will be,"
   in order that the passage of Scripture might be fulfilled that says:
      They divided my garments among them,
         and for my vesture they cast lots.

This is what the soldiers did.

[25] Standing by the cross of Jesus were his mother
and his mother's sister, Mary the wife of Clopas,
and Mary of Magdala.
[26] When Jesus saw his mother and the disciple there whom he loved
he said to his mother, "Woman, behold, your son."
[27] Then he said to the disciple,
"Behold, your mother."
And from that hour the disciple took her into his home.

[28] After this, aware that everything was now finished,
in order that the Scripture might be fulfilled,
Jesus said, "I thirst."
[29] There was a vessel filled with common wine.
So they put a sponge soaked in wine on a sprig of hyssop
and put it up to his mouth.
[30] When Jesus had taken the wine, he said,
"It is finished."
And bowing his head, he handed over the spirit.

[31] Now since it was preparation day,
in order that the bodies might not remain
on the cross on the sabbath,
for the sabbath day of that week was a solemn one,
the Jews asked Pilate that their legs be broken
and that they be taken down.
[32] So the soldiers came and broke the legs of the first
and then of the other one who was crucified with Jesus.
[33] But when they came to Jesus and saw that he was already dead,
they did not break his legs,
[34] but one soldier thrust his lance into his side,
and immediately blood and water flowed out.
[35] An eyewitness has testified, and his testimony is true;
he knows that he is speaking the truth,
so that you also may come to believe.
[36] For this happened so that the Scripture passage might be fulfilled:
Not a bone of it will be broken.
[37] And again another passage says:
They will look upon him whom they have pierced.

[38] After this, Joseph of Arimathea,
secretly a disciple of Jesus for fear of the Jews,
asked Pilate if he could remove the body of Jesus.
And Pilate permitted it.
So he came and took his body.

[39]Nicodemus, the one who had first come to him at night,
    also came bringing a mixture of myrrh and aloes
    weighing about one hundred pounds.
[40]They took the body of Jesus
    and bound it with burial cloths along with the spices,
    according to the Jewish burial custom.
[41]Now in the place where he had been crucified there was a garden,
    and in the garden a new tomb, in which no one had yet been buried.
[42]So they laid Jesus there because of the Jewish preparation day;
    for the tomb was close by.

The longest section from the Gospel of John contained within the lectionary is the passion narrative, which is read during all three cycles on Good Friday. Since the passion narrative presents the evangelist's account of how Jesus was arrested, convicted, executed, and buried, it relates directly to the issue of Jewish involvement in Jesus' death. The preacher and catechist must always keep in mind that, as we discussed in the Introduction, the gospel narratives are a mixture of history from the life of Jesus together with later theological reflection. Therefore, as we examine John's account of Jesus' passion, we must be aware that the historical remembrances preserved within it have been reshaped by John's theology and the situation of the Johannine community. In short, we cannot read John's passion as if we were reading a modern biography of Jesus.

This has a direct bearing on how we understand the circumstances of Jesus' death. Since the Second Vatican Council, Catholics are forbidden to rest the responsibility for Jesus' death on all the Jewish people of Jesus' day or of our own time (*Nostra Aetate*, #4). Yet there are some striking passages in John's passion account that could lead the ordinary reader to find support for just such beliefs. The preacher or catechist, then, bears a serious responsibility to proclaim the good news of John's passion narrative without supporting false and offensive explanations for Jesus' death.

THE HISTORICAL CIRCUMSTANCES OF JESUS' DEATH

Before examining John's presentation of Jesus' arrest and crucifixion, it will be helpful to outline what historical factors can be uncovered to explain this brutal execution. There is no doubt that Jesus died by a Roman form of execution: crucifixion. The title that all four gospels assert was posted on the cross, "The King of the Jews," indicates that the charge on which he was condemned by the Romans was a political rather than a religious one. With one exception, only the Roman governor had the authority to sentence anyone to death. Rome did allow the Temple authorities to execute any Gentile who transgressed certain areas of the Temple. But any other execution, including that of Jesus, could only be carried out through Roman auspices. The retort of the Temple authorities to Pilate, "We do not have the right to execute anyone" (18:31), is historically accurate. Roman involvement in Jesus' death is central and certain.

However, it is likely that some Jews were also involved. What was their motivation? Why would any Jew desire to turn over a fellow Jew to the destructive power of Rome? A variety of reasons for Jewish involvement has been suggested by those who attempt to uncover the circumstances of Jesus' crucifixion. It has been suggested that certain Jews were outraged at Jesus' teaching or jealous over his popularity. Another theory posits the corruption of those in authority as the cause of Jesus' death. None of these motives are historically probable. Various Jews in Jesus' time were outraged at the teaching and actions of other Jews. It was not, however, common practice to hand over their opponents to the Romans for execution. Nor, we might add, would the Roman governor be inclined to involve himself in taking sides in Jewish theological debates. Disagreement over Jesus' teaching and practice would not on its own lead to his execution.

As to the charge of jealousy, it would be a historical stretch to imagine that the Temple authorities would be envious of Jesus' limited influence and small band of followers. Christians honor Jesus in the light of his resurrection, proclaiming him as the unique Savior of the world. In the historical mix of first-century Judaism, however, Jesus and his followers were one movement among many and would not pose any serious threat to those in authority.

What of the charge that the Temple leadership was simply corrupt and motivated by evil intent? Some nefarious people can be found in every time and place. But to posit villainy as the cause for Jesus' death levels a charge with little historical justification. Joseph Caiaphas, who was high priest during Jesus' arrest and execution, was by all accounts a rather successful and respected official. He served seventeen years, longer than any other high priest under Roman authority.

Rather than involving ourselves in the merits and liabilities of these hypothetical motivations, we can identify a reason for Jewish involvement that is both historically reliable and persuasive. The Temple leadership participated in Jesus' death simply because they saw him as a threat to public order. As we saw in the Introduction, such a threat would undermine their forced alliance with the governor to keep the Roman peace. It must be remembered that Jesus was executed at Passover time. Such Jewish festivals were times at which Jerusalem was filled with pilgrims. The possibility of civil unrest was high. The Roman governor was counting on the Temple authorities to maintain order, and their jobs depended upon meeting that expectation.

All four gospels report that Jesus was involved in turning over some tables in the Temple. When this disruptive action was linked to reports that Jesus was associated with a small band of followers who had entered the holy city with a public display, the Temple authorities would have sufficient reason to notify Pilate. All that would be historically necessary for them to take such an action was their concern that his activities might spark public unrest. Pilate for his part would quickly sentence such an accused troublemaker to death. Life was cheap in occupied Judea, especially when the execution might prevent a disturbance that would endanger the governor's own standing before the emperor.

The central historical cause for Jesus' death, then, can be briefly stated: He was perceived by Pilate and by the Temple leadership allied with Pilate as a threat to civil order. Execution followed as it would for any Jew who was so perceived. The Temple authorities may well have disagreed with aspects of Jesus' teaching. They may have questioned his origins or his motives. But they knew that such concerns would not have mattered to Pilate. However, when Jesus was identified as a potential threat to Roman peace, the forced alliance between Pilate and the Temple authorities swung into action. It was then that the way was opened to the cross.

It should be added here that, as we move away from the historical circumstances of Jesus' death in stage one of the gospel tradition, there is a general tendency in all four gospels (stage three) to reduce the amount of Roman involvement in Jesus' crucifixion and to increase Jewish responsibility. In the gospels the initiative for Jesus' crucifixion and its driving force are often assigned to the Temple leadership. The gospels do not reveal that the swift execution of perceived troublemakers was a demand of the Roman occupying forces. Pilate is frequently portrayed as a weak, vacillating man who sentences Jesus to death because he is intimidated by the Temple leadership. This is a far different Pilate than the one presented to us by Josephus, who reports several incidents in which Pilate freely exercises his authority with conviction and brutality (*Antiquities* XVIII, 3, 2 and 4, 2; *War* II, 9, 4). Therefore, the kinder, more introspective Pilate seems to be the creation of the early church, which is inclined to portray Roman officials as pawns in the hands of the Temple authorities.

Why would such a description prove attractive to the evangelists? They were taking their audiences into consideration. As the Christian movement spread, it found little response from Jewish groups. Gentiles, however, entered in great numbers. Christian missionaries were therefore eager to have the death of Jesus less associated with Gentile/Roman power. This explains the penchant in the gospels to enlarge Jewish involvement and diminish the agency of Roman forces.

Care must be taken in the use of the passion narratives lest we affirm the false impression that the primary responsibility for Jesus' death lies in the hands of the Temple authorities, with Pilate as an innocent bystander. At its worst such careless treatment of these texts can seem to support the collective responsibility of the Jewish people for the death of Jesus.

As we proceed now to examine John's passion narrative, we will discover that John uses a variety of terms to describe Jewish involvement in Jesus' death. Some of these terms seem to enlarge Jewish responsibility beyond that of the Temple leadership, giving the impression that Jesus' death was organized and supported by the Jewish people as a whole. Because such an impression has led to disastrous consequences throughout history, it has been officially rejected by the Catholic Church (*Nostra Aetate*, #4). I will frequently argue that the text is not referring to the whole Jewish people but rather to some of their leaders. When these arguments are presented, the reader must recall two further points, namely, that the Temple leaders in question were themselves compromised by their forced alliance with Rome and that the pervasive and contaminating influence of Roman imperialism is not readily apparent in John's narrative. In other words, even when we are able to limit Jewish involvement in Jesus' death to the Temple leadership, it must be remembered that such leaders were not acting as independent authorities in their own land but as officials tied to the imposed interests of the Roman state. It is only when these factors are appreciated that the preacher will be able to recognize the historical realities that underlie John's passion account and proclaim the gospel message without perpetuating false and destructive conclusions.

In the following pages I will first attempt to cue the preacher or catechist to the opportunities within John's passion narrative to emphasize a more historically accurate understanding of Roman and Jewish involvement in Jesus' suffering and death. I will then discuss those characteristics that have the potential to foster an inaccurate and harmful anti-Judaism.

POSITIVE FACTORS TOWARD JEWS AND JUDAISM IN JOHN'S PRESENTATION OF JESUS' PASSION AND DEATH

There is no official hearing before the Sanhedrin in the passion of John. The inquiry before sending Jesus to Pilate is reduced to a hearing before Annas (18:19–24) and one before Caiaphas, which is not specifically described (18:24, 28). Compared to the Synoptic gospels, then, the involvement by Temple authorities in John's passion narrative is less formal and less public. This fact significantly lessens the impression of Jewish responsibility for Jesus' death.

The abuse of Jesus while in Jewish hands is limited in John. In Mark (14:65) and Matthew (26:67–68), Jesus is insulted and struck by a number of people in the very presence of the Sanhedrin and possibly by members of the council itself. Luke (22:63–65) has those who were holding Jesus abuse him before the council meets. In John the Jewish abuse of Jesus is confined to the action of one person, and it consists of a single blow (18:22).

The abuse of Jesus on the cross is also absent in John. In Mark (15:29–32) and Matthew (27:39–44), passersby, the chief priests, the scribes and elders, and the two robbers crucified with Jesus all taunt him. In Luke (23:35–39) the taunts are limited to only the authorities, the soldiers, and one of the robbers. In John the mocking of Jesus on the cross does not occur. Since the majority of those who taunted Jesus in the Synoptic accounts were Jewish, this particular negative presentation of Jews is avoided in John.

The passion account in John ends with a positive Jewish image. Two Jewish believers in Jesus ask for his body in order to provide a Jewish burial (19:38–42). Joseph of Arimathea appears in all four gospels to request Jesus' body. In John he is joined by Nicodemus, who assists in the burial. Joseph is said to be a secret disciple of Jesus (19:38) and the reader realizes that Nicodemus has previously spoken in Jesus' favor before the Pharisees (7:50–51). Although the faith of both men seems tentative and weak, their action of kindness toward Jesus ends the passion narrative with a thrust positive to Jews and Judaism.

Within the passion narrative John shows a greater willingness than the Synoptics in admitting Roman responsibility for the death of Jesus. Because there is no Sanhedrin session in John's passion, the emphasis in John falls on the trial before Pilate. Moreover, although the religious issue of Jesus' identity is mentioned in the accusations before Pilate (19:7), the primary issue before Pilate is a political one: whether Jesus is the king of the Jews (18:33, 37, 39; 19:3, 12, 14, 19, 21). This political orientation is confirmed later in the account when the chief priests declare their opposition to Jesus in political terms: "We have no king but Caesar!" (19:15).

John is also the only gospel that mentions Roman involvement in the arrest of Jesus. In the Synoptics Jesus is arrested by a crowd sent from the chief priests, scribes, and elders. John describes the arrest differently. He claims that Judas arrived with "a band of soldiers and guards from the chief priests and the Pharisees" (18:3). The term translated "band of soldiers" is in Greek *speira*, which is literally "cohort" and always refers to Roman soldiers. At the end of the arrest scene (18:12), the Greek word for "tribune" is *chiliarchos*, another Roman military term. Moreover, the clear contrast between the soldiers with their officer and "the Jewish guards" leaves no doubt that John sees the soldiers as Roman.

A Roman cohort consisted of six hundred soldiers. To assume that such a large force was sent out to arrest a single suspect appears unlikely. Perhaps John is being imprecise in his military terminology. What is more likely is that the evangelist is presenting a symbolic image to show Jesus' power over both Roman and Jewish forces — they both fall to the ground before him (18:6). Yet even though the presence of Roman forces here might be symbolic, the symbolism can be used to correct a historical imbalance. The Roman involvement in this scene is a reminder that historically Jesus could not have been crucified without full and deliberate Roman participation. As we have discussed above, the gospels imply that the Roman authorities were manipulated, deceived, or intimidated by Jewish forces. However, the political situation at the time of Jesus' arrest was determined primarily by the aims of Roman imperial policy, in which policy the Jewish Temple leadership was assigned a supporting role.

In summary, the passion narrative of John seems in many ways more favorable to Jews than the Synoptic accounts. There is no official meeting of the Sanhedrin. There is significantly less abuse of Jesus by Jews during the passion. Roman involvement is heightened in both the arrest of Jesus and the prominence given to the trial before Pilate. Finally, two weak but kindly Jewish disciples close the passion by providing Jesus with a burial according to traditional Jewish customs.

NEGATIVE FACTORS TOWARD JEWS AND JUDAISM IN JOHN'S PRESENTATION OF JESUS' PASSION AND DEATH

Despite the positive tendencies mentioned above, a number of other elements of John's passion narrative are more negative to Jews and Judaism than those in the Synoptic accounts. Remarkably enough, the first of these is one that has just been described among the positive factors: the trial before Pilate. As we have seen, John's emphasis on this trial rather than on the formal session of the Sanhedrin that is presented in Matthew, Mark, and Luke lessens the emphasis on Jewish involvement. In John, the only formal trial is a Roman one. Yet when the trial before Pilate is examined in terms of its meaning and structure, it is questionable whether the Jewish characters are presented any more positively than in the Synoptics.

The Roman trial of Jesus is presented in such a way that the Jewish characters play a major role. Pilate moves back and forth in an elaborate pattern between quiet conversations with Jesus inside the praetorium and ever-louder confrontations with Jesus' accusers in the outside court. The careful plotting of the scenes betrays a conscious literary structure on the part of the evangelist to emphasize Pilate's struggle to choose between Jesus and his opponents. The Jewish characters are, therefore, a consistent component of the Roman trial. They deliver Jesus to Pilate (18:28), insist he is a criminal (18:30), reject

Jesus for Barabbas (18:40), call for his death (19:6–7, 15), and claim they have no king but Caesar (19:15).

The Jewish opposition argues with Pilate, "We do not have the right to execute anyone" (18:31). At first, this conviction—which is expressed only in John—seems to lessen Jewish responsibility by its claim that the death penalty could be imposed only by Roman authority. However, when the statement is read in light of John's overall narrative, it becomes a means to express a Jewish demand, making Jews responsible for Jesus' death, even though crucifixion was a Roman form of execution.

Therefore, the trial before Pilate in John cannot be used unambiguously to argue for a more favorable presentation of Jewish involvement in the death of Jesus. Because the trial centers so clearly on the choice of Pilate between Jesus and his accusers, the real motivators of Jesus' death and the true villains of the scene are the Jewish leaders. Even though the Roman trial replaces the Sanhedrin hearings of the Synoptics, the Jewish opposition remains a constitutive element of the Johannine trial scene and indeed its guiding force.

An additional twist that intensifies Jewish responsibility in John's passion account occurs after the end of the trial. In John 19:15c–18, note the flow of the pronouns, seemingly following a reference to the chief priests (emphases added):

> The *chief priests* answered, "We have no king but Caesar." Then he [Pilate] handed him over to *them* to be crucified.
> So *they* took Jesus, and, carrying the cross himself, he went out to what is called the Place of the Skull, in Hebrew, Golgotha. There *they* crucified him, and with him two others, one on either side, with Jesus in the middle.

By omitting any new reference to the agents of the crucifixion, John gives the initial impression that Pilate handed Jesus over to the chief priests so that *they* might crucify him. By 19:19 this impression is corrected. There John reports a dispute between Pilate and the chief priests over the title affixed to the cross. This clearly indicates Roman control of the crucifixion. Nevertheless, the initial impression given at the end of the trial is that Jesus was given over into Jewish hands.

The negative factors we have already considered derive from context and implication. However, when we examine the manner in which John identifies Jesus' opponents in the passion narrative, the adverse impressions become more explicit. In 18:3 we are told that the group that came to arrest Jesus included guards who were sent from the chief priests and the Pharisees. The mention of the Pharisees in this scene is unusual. Besides one mention of them in Matthew 27:62, this is the only time in any canonical gospel that the Pharisees are associated with the events of Jesus' passion. Their presence in Matthew may have resulted from a popular story, probably about Jesus' resurrection, that Matthew included in his Gospel. This story might well have developed rather late in the gospel tradition, when Matthew's community was already struggling with opponents of a Pharisaic persuasion. This would explain the unusual appearance of the Pharisees in Matthew's passion account.

John, finding his community also in a struggle with Pharisaic opponents, may have inserted this one reference to the Pharisees into his arrest scene in order to render the opposition to Jesus more relevant to his own situation. Although the Pharisees are frequently presented as the opponents of Jesus in the gospels' accounts of his ministry, their absence in the passion narratives (with these two exceptions) is significant. It strongly indicates that they were not a Jewish group associated with the death of Jesus in the historical remembrances passed down to the gospel writers.

The one mention of the Pharisees occurs early in John's passion account. No sooner do they depart, however, than a more serious problem emerges: the frequent polemical use of *hoi Ioudaioi*. In 18:3 we were told that Judas brought "a band of soldiers and guards from the *chief priests* and the *Pharisees*." By 18:12, however, this group has become "the Jewish guards" or "the guards of the Jews." This is the first time in the passion narrative that *hoi Ioudaioi* is used. Typical of the polemical use (see Introduction), it here replaces more specific terms for Jesus' opponents (the chief priests and Pharisees). This replacement begins to happen with increasing frequency within the passion narrative. From this point on, the precision of terms referring to Jesus' opponents starts to slip. Distinctions among the various agents within the passion become muddled under the cover of the all-embracing term, *hoi Ioudaioi*.

Hoi Ioudaioi is used twenty-two times in John's passion narrative. Of these, six times (18:33, 39; 19:3, 19, 21b, 21c) it is part of the title associated with Jesus in all the gospels, "the King of the Jews."

These six occurrences are not polemical. There are another six occurrences when *hoi Ioudaioi* is used in a neutral sense. Here the phrase refers to those who worship in the Temple (18:20), those who read the inscription on the cross (19:20), the nationality of a person (18:35), of leaders (19:21a), of burial customs (19:40), or of a feast (19:42). In these six uses *hoi Ioudaioi* is used to identify rather than to denigrate.

We have already noted the use of *hoi Ioudaioi* in 18:12, where it covers over the referent to the chief priests and the Pharisees. The remaining nine occurrences of *hoi Ioudaioi* are classic polemical uses. All of them are best understood as replacements for the Temple authorities in Jerusalem. In 18:14 we are told that Caiaphas was the one who had advised *hoi Ioudaioi* that it was better to have one person die for the people. Earlier in the Gospel (11:45–53) Caiaphas gave that advice before the Sanhedrin. It is likely, then, that *hoi Ioudaioi* has been used in 18:14 to replace a reference to that religious body.

In 18:28 John says, "Then *they* brought Jesus from Caiaphas to the praetorium." No proper subject is specified. The careful reader will follow back and realize that the chief priests and their attendants are intended. But the next time a subject is given (18:31), Pilate is arguing with *hoi Ioudaioi*. When this is translated as "the Jews" (as in the lectionary), the impression is given that the entire trial scene is between Pilate and the Jewish people rather than between Pilate and the chief priests. This is surely the most dangerous section in John's passion narrative, for an unreflective understanding of it would lead the reader to believe that the whole Jewish people plotted and managed Jesus' sentence of death. Indeed there are times when the chief priests rise again into view. In 19:6 it is the chief priests and the police who cry out for crucifixion, and in 19:15 it is the chief priests who assert that they have no king but Caesar. Yet, in the rest of the trial scene, *hoi Ioudaioi* covers the activity of the chief priests (18:38; 19:7, 12, 14). Thus it could appear that somehow the entire Jewish population is involved. Pilate seems to say as much when he remarks to Jesus, "Your own nation and the chief priests handed you over to me" (18:35). Jesus, in his response to Pilate (18:36), appears to agree when he talks about being handed over to *hoi Ioudaioi*.

On the level of Jesus' historical trial, it makes little sense to charge that Jesus' "nation" handed him over. But how often do listeners stop to consider that implausibility? Without reflection, such verses generate an impression that Jesus was not a part of the Jewish nation and that somehow all Jews in Jesus' time were involved in handing him over. It is easy to forget that some of the Temple leadership in forced alliance with Pilate may have indeed handed him over, but certainly not the Jewish people as a whole. When we understand John's tendency to equate the opponents of his own time with the Temple leadership, we can appreciate why this dialogue is written as it is. Yet without that understanding, the harmful effects of the passage may well run unchecked.

The polemical use of *hoi Ioudaioi* extends beyond the trial of Jesus. When a request is made of Pilate to have the legs of those crucified broken so that the bodies would not remain on the crosses during the Sabbath, we are told *hoi Ioudaioi* made the request (19:31). When *hoi Ioudaioi* is translated as "the Jews," this verse cannot be understood as referring to "all Jews." There is no way to imagine the whole nation approaching Pilate. Here again we clearly have *hoi Ioudaioi* standing in for the Temple authorities who were aligned with Pilate. Later, when Joseph of Arimathea is said to be a secret disciple of Jesus "for fear of *hoi Ioudaioi*" (19:38), the same point can be made. How can Joseph be afraid of "the Jews" when he is Jewish himself? Again we must understand here a subgroup of Jews, such as the chief priests, whose position was dependent upon keeping the Roman peace.

Therefore, the scope of responsibility for Jesus' death and the scope of the polemic of the passion narrative are significantly widened by John's use of *hoi Ioudaioi*. In a translation without nuance, the anti-Jewish potential of the passion narrative is immensely increased because the reader is left with the impression that Jesus was put to death not by the chief priests nor the Pharisees nor the crowds nor even the Romans—but simply by "the Jews."

PREACHING JOHN'S PASSION NARRATIVE

Because of the length and richness of John's passion account, the preacher or catechist can focus on many important truths within the text. The primary focus of any preaching should be the good news of Jesus' saving death for our salvation. It would be tedious, and perhaps improper, to include within the preaching a discussion of the complex nature of John's passion that we have just discussed. What the preacher can do, however, is to assure that the anti-Jewish potential within the text is minimized. This can be achieved in a number of ways.

First, the preacher or catechist should be careful not to repeat the polemical use of *hoi Ioudaioi* as he or she is recalling a scene from the passion. Using phrases such as "Jesus' accusers" or "the Temple authorities" will more accurately capture the reference of *hoi Ioudaioi* and at the same time limit the false impression of widespread Jewish responsibility.

Second, since the preacher is aware that the polemical use of *hoi Ioudaioi* in the passion can give the impression of involvement of the whole Jewish people in Jesus' death, it should be stated clearly in the preaching that we as Christians do not believe that the Jewish people are responsible then or now for Jesus' crucifixion. This is simply restating the official teaching of *Nostra Aetate*, #4, and there could be no better time to do it. It need not be a major point of the preaching or catechesis. However, mentioning it succinctly at some point will go a long way in undercutting the perception of mass Jewish responsibility in the minds of those in our assemblies.

Third, the preacher could use the increased recognition of Roman involvement in John's passion narrative to correct the overly innocent presentation of Roman responsibility that the other gospels portray. It could be asserted in preaching that Jesus' crucifixion did not result primarily from disputes over his teaching but rather from the overriding concern of the Roman Empire to eliminate any person whose presence could spark the unrest of an oppressed populace.

Fourth, the preacher could explore the possibility of integrating into the preaching one of the positive points discussed above. For example, it could prove helpful to mention that John probably gives us a more historically accurate presentation of Jesus' interrogation before the Jewish authorities by omitting the Sanhedrin session of the Synoptics with its accompanying mockery and abuse of Jesus. Also, the burial scene could be used to present the faithfulness and love of discipleship as well as Jesus' Jewish heritage.

Finally, opportunities to discuss the issue of Jewish responsibility in Jesus' death at greater length outside of the preaching event should be encouraged. As Holy Week approaches, a fuller understanding of the historical circumstances of Jesus' crucifixion and the characteristics of John's narration could be promoted through adult-

education sessions, the catechesis of those preparing for baptism, and
articles in the parish bulletin or newsletter.

THE DEATH OF CHRIST AND THE DEICIDE ACCUSATION

The New Testament text clearly shows that Pontius Pilate, the governor or prefect of Judea, ordered Jesus' death. But the response
through the centuries has been quite different. The Reverend
Daniel J. Harrington writes in his essay, "Who Killed Jesus?":

> "Who Killed Jesus?" This simple question needs and deserves
> a careful answer. Throughout the centuries some have
> responded that the Jews killed Jesus, and therefore they are a
> "deicide" people. The word "deicide" means to kill God.
> Since Jesus is divine and since the Jews killed Jesus, there-
> fore they must be a deicide people. This "logic" sometimes
> gives Christians a rationale and a motive for killing Jews. One
> result of this tradition was the Nazi Holocaust or *Shoah*. The
> hideous results of a careless answer to a simple question
> proved the need for taking the issue with utmost seriousness.

This negative view of the role of Jews in the passion of Christ is
evident in European art as well as in passion plays. European cathe-
drals or palaces often show in stained-glass windows or in sculp-
tures a teaching of contempt and a theological denial of Judaism,
proclaiming Jews as the killers of Jesus. In Italy, for example, in the
church in Urbino, a woman is shown stealing the host and handing
it over to a Jewish pawnbroker for its destruction. They are discovered and burned at the stake. In a classic of Spanish literature, *Las
Cantigas de Santa Maria,* a compilation of poetry and music by
Alfonso X of Castile (1252–84), there are six pictures illustrating a
legend about the theft by a Jew (under the inspiration of a devil) of
a picture of the Virgin Mary. A Christian and his wife find the picture
and wash it clean. The couple gives the picture a place of honor in
their home and pilgrims come and pay homage to the holy picture.

The church fathers transformed the theological teaching of contempt into the deicide accusation.

The third-century church father Cyprian, in his *Three Books of
Testimonies Against the Jews,* wrote:

> There is a new dispensation and a New Law with abrogation of
> the Law of Moses and the Holy Temple. The Man of Righteous-

ness was put to death by the Jews; they fastened him to the cross. Now the peoplehood of the Jews has been canceled; the destruction of Jerusalem was a judgment upon them; the Gentiles rather than the Jews will inherit the Kingdom....

Melito of Sardis, who died ca. 190 CE, castigated Israel for its rejection of Jesus in his Homily of Pascha:

For him who the Gentiles worshipped and uncircumcised people admired and foreigners glorified, over whom even Pilate washed his hands, you killed at the great feast. Bitter therefore for you is the feast of unleavened bread.... Bitter for you are the nails you sharpened, bitter for you the tongue you incited, bitter for you the false witnesses you instructed...bitter for you Judas whom you hired, bitter for you Herod whom you followed, bitter for you Caiaphas whom you trusted,...bitter for you the hands you bloodied; you killed your Lord in the middle of Jerusalem.

...[T]he King of Israel has been put to death by an Israelite right hand. O unprecedented murder! Unprecedented crime!

In Melito's Homily, Pilate disappears from the scene and the Jewish people take center stage. It is the deicide accusation at its best theological formulation.

More examples of the deicide accusation can be found in Irenaeus (ca. 130–200 CE), Origen (ca. 185–254 CE), and especially in John Chrysostom (ca. 347–407 CE).

Father Harrington writes in his study:

The best clue toward determining who killed Jesus is the mode of Jesus' death—by crucifixion. In Jesus' time, crucifixion was Roman punishment inflicted mainly on slaves and revolutionaries. Crucifixion was a cruel and public way to die. As a public punishment, it was meant to shame the one being executed and to deter the onlookers from doing what he has done.

Father Harrington adds:

The official who had the power to execute Jesus by crucifixion was the Roman governor or prefect. In Jesus' time the prefect was Pontius Pilate, who held that position between A.D. 26 and 36. Jesus was put to death "under Pontius Pilate" around

A.D. 30. Although the gospels present Pilate as indecisive and somewhat concerned for Jesus' case, the Alexandrian Jewish writer, Philo, a contemporary of Jesus, described him as "inflexible, merciless, and obstinate."

Though some Christians continue to blame Jews for Jesus' death, it is still a matter that gnaws at the conscience of other Christians. It is reflected in the responses of Christian leaders. New Testament scholar Episcopal Bishop Frederick H. Borsch, commenting on deicide accusations, said:

It tells us we continue to have a very important task in front of us. One of the central tasks for Christianity is to turn away from any kind of history in its past which has been anti-Semitic, or allows that to be promoted in any way.

The point is simple: For two thousand years, church teaching and practice fostered an understanding of Jews and Judaism that helped create the atmosphere that made the Shoah possible.

Christianity in the last fifty years has reckoned with the theological anti-Judaism that nurtured civilization for centuries. The Holocaust is painfully central in such a reconsideration of the Christian soul. Official documents from nearly all Christian churches have expressed pain, asking for forgiveness and reconciliation. These expressions of sincerest repentance still need further implementation at pew level to educate Christians of the sin of the deicide accusation in order to avoid recent expressions accusing Jews of killing Jesus.

The Bishops' Committee on the Liturgy of the National Conference of Catholic Bishops in their document, *God's Mercy Endures Forever*, clearly states the need to overcome anti-Judaism and the deicide accusation:

21. Because of the tragic history of the "Christ-killer" charge as providing a rallying cry for anti-Semitism over the centuries, a strong and careful homiletic stance is necessary to combat its lingering effects today. Homilists and catechists should seek to provide a proper context for the proclamation of the Passion narratives. A particularly useful and detailed discussion of the theological and historical principles involved in presentations of the passions can be found in *Criteria for the Evaluation of Dramatizations of the Passion* issued by the

Bishops' Committee for Ecumenical and Interreligious Affairs (March 1988).

22. The message of the liturgy in proclaiming the Passion narratives in full is to enable the assembly to see vividly the love of Christ for each person, despite their sins, a love that even death could not vanquish. "Christ in his boundless love freely underwent his passion and death because of the sins of all so that all might attain salvation" (*Nostra Aetate,* No. 4). To the extent that Christians over the centuries made Jews the scapegoat for Christ's death, they drew themselves away from the paschal mystery. For it is only by dying to one's sins that we can hope to rise with Christ to new life. This is a central truth of the Catholic faith stated by the *Catechism* of the Council of Trent in the sixteenth century and reaffirmed by the 1985 *Notes* (No. 30).

This call to reckoning and reconciliation is the best response to the deicide charge, requiring a pervasive and systematic educational implementation at the pew level. This theological implementation would, over time, eliminate the deicide accusation in the mind and heart of Christians.

Rabbinic Notes on the Account of the Death of Jesus: John 18:1—19:42

18:12, 22: So the soldiers, their officer, and the Jewish police arrested Jesus and bound him.... When he had said this, one of the police standing nearby struck Jesus on the face, saying, "Is that how you answer the high priest ?"

Some may ask, "Who were these Jewish 'guards' or 'police' mentioned in the narrative of the passion? Did Jews have a security force of their own? Wasn't their treatment of Jesus cruel? The answer is yes, there was a Jewish police force that kept order in the Temple, much like today there are separate religious police in Mecca, for example, or even the Swiss Guard at the Vatican who help to manage huge numbers of annual pilgrims in such holy places. The apparent harshness of the guard in John 18:22 should not be seen as anything other than typical police behavior against alleged dissidents; there was no anti-Judaism in such an act, but merely a strict control of speech and acts in the presence of officials. In effect, such a guard could have struck anyone who was perceived, as Jesus was or the two brigands eventually crucified alongside him, as being a criminal under interrogation.

18:31: Pilate said to them, "Take him yourselves and judge him according to your law." The Jews replied, "We are not permitted to put anyone to death."

In addition to the Roman proscription against subordinated societies like Israel administering the death penalty, the Jewish law itself set the most demanding standards for trial that might lead to execution. By "law" here is meant the jurisprudence found in biblical law and Sanhedrin case law as reflected in the Mishnah, *Sanhedrin,* 4. There, we find an outline of the proper procedures for a capital trial. By such standards, Annas and Caiaphas could not have condemned Jesus to death. It is only because they abandoned authentic Jewish practice in this area—and any allegiance to King Herod (cf. John 19:1)—that they could have sent Jesus to the Roman governor in the first place. Further, it must be remembered that both Annas and Caiaphas owed their continuing appointments as high priests to Pontius Pilate directly, and no longer to their Temple confreres. As a result, the statement at 18:31 in John's Gospel should never be read as a pretext for anti-Judaism, where many Christian commentators have alleged that the actions of Annas and Caiaphas were representative of the Jewish people and of authentic Jewish law.

A brief note on the person and role of Pontius Pilate may also be of interest. Pontius Pilate was apparently appointed the governor of Judea by Tiberius Caesar for a term that lasted from 26 CE to 36 CE. He was fired by the emperor in 36 CE, after being summoned to Rome due to frequent complaints of his cruel treatment of the Jews. Philo (*De legatione ad Gaium,* 38) and Josephus (*Antiquities,* 18,3,1), two ancient Jewish historians, describe Pilate as a man without any human feeling. His role here in John's Gospel typifies the kind of Roman cynicism that came to be the expected order of the day: sarcastically taunting the locals to take matters into their own hands, either as a pretext for later Roman intervention or as proof of their innate inferiority to Roman law and character. It must always be kept in mind that the Roman occupation of Israel was a complete one: No religious practice was permitted that did not conform to Roman political interests in the region. Hence, from the appointment of the high priests in the Temple to the decision to carry out the death penalty against any Jew, the Roman authorities remained clearly in charge. As a result, any move by Pilate to appear deferential to the Jews—even during Passover—must be viewed with suspicion. The ultimate proof of Pilate's manipulative character is the choice he offers to the Jews as a token of Roman mercy during Passover: the release of Barabbas, a known insurrectionist and murderer, or the death of Jesus. From first to last, the role of Pilate with respect to Jesus must be understood as a political one in which Pilate is constantly weighing the interests of Rome and his own administration against the requests of the Jews, whom he detests. It is only by Pilate's authority that Jesus could be put to death, as attested to in the complaint of the high priests over the sign hung above Jesus' head on the cross (cf. Mark 15:26, John 19:19–22)—a sign whose *titulus* (or stated reason for the execution of the criminal) was calculated to gall the same high priests who owed Pilate for their high office in the Temple and the safeguarding of their personal power.

19:31: Since it was the day of Preparation, the Jews did not want the bodies left on the cross during the sabbath, especially because that sabbath was a day of great solemnity. So they asked Pilate to have the legs of the crucified men broken and the bodies removed.
The probable reason for Jewish concern about the bodies of Christ and the criminals being left on their crosses was a concern for following the Jewish practice of immediate burial after death. See Deuteronomy 21:23, where those hung on a tree were never to be left there overnight. In the Talmud at *Baba Kava* 82b, such burials are encouraged in order to avoid what Deuteronomy refers to as "defilement of the land" on which the executed body rests. The reason for this is simple: In Jewish thought, the human body is the image of God who created it. Its degradation following death becomes a degradation of the image of the Creator and, hence, a defilement of the land that holds it (see the *Chumash,* the medieval rabbinic commentary on Deuteronomy, for greater detail). Often, this verse has been misread as a statement of Jewish disdain for the bodies of executed criminals, and of Jesus' body in particular, as somehow marring the celebration of the coming Sabbath. In fact, however, the needed burials were a concern for the reasons given above, whether the Sabbath was to follow the next day or not.

A final note on the breaking of the leg bones of the criminals may be in order. The obvious reason given for this practice was that broken legs would hasten death for the crucified, since it meant that they could no longer continue to raise themselves up against the back of their crosses in order to breathe; in effect, they suffocated by having their full weight pull them down so low that breathing became impossible. However, the breaking of the legs would cause a disfigurement to the bodies—a shameful and scandalous way in which to treat the human body as the image of the Creator. Such a disfigurement was thought by many to stand in the way of the resurrection. It is therefore important to note that John's Gospel carefully states that when it came to Jesus, the soldiers did not break his bones, but instead pierced him with a lance (cf. John 19:31–37) as if to avoid the shame of any broken bones, subtly intended to signal the loss of a potential resurrection.

5
The Second Sunday of Easter, Cycles A, B, C • John 20:19–31

20:19On the evening of that first day of the week,
    when the doors were locked, where the disciples were,
    for fear of the Jews,
    Jesus came and stood in their midst
    and said to them, "Peace be with you."
20When he had said this, he showed them his hands and his side.
The disciples rejoiced when they saw the Lord.
21Jesus said to them again, "Peace be with you.
As the Father has sent me, so I send you."
22And when he had said this, he breathed on them and said to them,
    "Receive the Holy Spirit.
23Whose sins you forgive are forgiven them,
    and whose sins you retain are retained."

24Thomas, called Didymus, one of the Twelve,
    was not with them when Jesus came.
25So the other disciples said to him, "We have seen the Lord."
But he said to them,
    "Unless I see the mark of the nails in his hands
    and put my finger into the nailmarks
    and put my hand into his side, I will not believe."

26Now a week later his disciples were again inside
    and Thomas was with them.
Jesus came, although the doors were locked,
    and stood in their midst and said, "Peace be with you."
27Then he said to Thomas, "Put your finger here and see my hands,
    and bring your hand and put it into my side,
    and do not be unbelieving, but believe."
28Thomas answered and said to him, "My Lord and my God!"
29Jesus said to him, "Have you come to believe because you have seen me?
Blessed are those who have not seen and have believed."

³⁰Now, Jesus did many other signs in the presence of his disciples
   that are not written in this book.
³¹But these are written that you may come to believe
   that Jesus is the Christ, the Son of God,
   and that through this belief you may have life in his name.

This account of Jesus' appearance to his disciples after the resurrection is used extensively within the Catholic lectionary. It is
assigned for all three years on the Sunday after Easter, and an abbrevi-
ated version (20:19–23) is read on Pentecost in Cycle A and is given
as an option for the gospel on Pentecost in cycles B and C. Therefore,
its strengths and its dangers will receive wide exposure. Its strengths
are many. The risen Christ comes to his fearful disciples and offers
them peace. Showing them the signs of his passion that have now
become the marks of his glory, he bestows his Spirit upon them and
commissions them to go forth into the world with the authority he
received from his Father. The disciple Thomas expresses the final and
fullest expression of Johannine Christology, "My Lord and my God"
(20:28). This provides an opportunity for Jesus to bless subsequent
disciples who will believe in him without the advantage of seeing as
Thomas did.

The potential danger in this passage for anti-Jewish bias centers
on verse 19. There we are told that the doors of the place were locked
for fear of *hoi Ioudaioi*. Although this phrase is usually translated "for
fear of the Jews" (as in the lectionary translation), that reference is
clearly too wide. All the disciples locked into the room were themselves Jewish. A subgroup of Jews—such as the authorities aligned
with Rome—must be understood.

It is easy to imagine why the disciples would have been afraid
after Jesus' crucifixion. They had been associated with one who was
publicly executed. It must be remembered, however, that the brutal
death of Jesus was a Roman action. Even though *hoi Ioudaioi* may
well point to those in the Temple leadership who were cooperating
with Rome, it was Roman power that the disciples would fear.
Therefore, the mention of a Jewish group in this verse is another
example of the Gospel's tendency to overemphasize the Jewish side
of the Roman-Temple alliance.

Moreover, this verse should not be used to conclude that the
Romans and high priests were involved in a search to locate and seize
Jesus' followers. We have no historical evidence to support attempts

to arrest the disciples of Jesus after his crucifixion. The Romans did not perceive Jesus' followers as supporting a military agenda. Had they such a suspicion, Pilate would not have rested until all those connected to Jesus were eliminated. Contrary to any such Roman action, we have every reason to believe that after Jesus' death his followers continued to live peacefully in Jerusalem and worship in the Temple. Luke affirms this scenario at the end of his Gospel (24:52–53).

John may have added the phrase, "for fear of *hoi Ioudaioi*," to an earlier postresurrection account. Postresurrectional accounts are usually characterized by a motif of fear or surprise (Mark 16:8; Matt 28:4, 5, 8, 10; Luke 24:5, 37). John may have inserted *hoi Ioudaioi* into this scene to reflect the fear of his own community arising from the struggle with the Pharisees at the end of the first century. The astute preacher or catechist could utilize this insertion for pastoral benefit. Mentioning how the fear of the Johannine community is reflected in this verse, the preacher could point to similar fears present in our lives today. Such a connection would be productive in at least two ways. Listeners would not only identify with the struggles and fears of an early Christian community but also avoid the bias that this verse could convey against the Jewish leaders of Jesus' day.

Rabbinic Notes on the First Day of the Week: John 20:19–31

20:19: When it was evening on that day, the first day of the week, and the doors of the house where the disciples had met were locked for fear of the Jews....
Several phrases in this verse will draw our reflection. First, the description of "the first day of week"—depending on how the evangelist is counting time since the appearance of Jesus following the resurrection scene—evokes an image of the "day of the Lord" in Isaiah 52:6. Originally, it seems that Jewish Christians (a name coined here to describe the followers of Jesus before they were separated from the synagogues) celebrated their memorial of Jesus at the *end of the Jewish Sabbath, by extending their prayer through all of Saturday night.* It is important for us to note that, in so doing, the point of reference for them was the Jewish Sabbath and not the resurrection day of Jesus per se (cf. Acts 2:46). It would appear that John is here speaking of the disciples—who, as observant Jews, have remained the full week in Jerusalem for the observance of the Passover—gathered at the end of the Sabbath, but now in fear "of the Jews." Who would these Jews be? As we have discussed above,

this phrase most likely refers to those in authority who have collaborated with the Romans on the persecution and death of Jesus. It could hardly refer to all Jews, since the disciples themselves are Jews and have remained among Jews for the entire week. Would it be too much to suggest that the reason they have hidden themselves away is because they have not assembled *as the followers of Jesus since his reappearance after death*? As observant individuals mixed in among the great crowds of Jerusalem, they would have nothing to fear; but as the followers of Jesus, somehow gathered in the same place, they could attract the attention of the Roman-backed Temple authority that had executed their master.

20:19: Jesus came and stood among them and said, "Peace be with you."
In Rabbinic Hebrew, "Peace to you" was a standard greeting, even used later as a way in which a rabbi or teacher would reveal his presence to his followers who were delighted to see him (cf. Judg 6:23 and Dan 10:19). Here, Jesus' greeting is very much that of a rabbi who greets his disciples, ready to engage them in the work of prayer or study.

20:22: When he had said this, he breathed on them and said to them, "Receive the Holy Spirit."
To some small degree, this verse might invoke the image of Genesis 2:7, where in both the Hebrew text and the Septuagint or Greek text, God fills Adam with his breath, which is life itself (cf. also Wis 15:11). But perhaps more importantly, this phrase is redolent of the steady practice among the prophets who would breathe upon their chosen disciples as they passed on the Spirit of prophecy given to them by God (cf. Deut 34:9 and 2 Kgs 2:9–10).

20:23: "If you forgive the sins of any, they are forgiven them; if you retain the sins of any, they are retained."
In many ways, this scene seems modeled on episodes such as are found in Isaiah 22:22, since Jesus here bestows his own authority over *binding* and *loosening* on membership and sins in the community of disciples who were to follow (cf. the prophetic style of his language at Mark 7:8). Jesus' statement resembles, to some degree, that found in Sirach 28:1, though stronger parallels are found in Qumran Judaism, where the head of the community is described as one who "loosens all the fetters that bind them, so that no one should be oppressed or broken in his congregation" (*Cairo Genizah,*13.9–10). Rabbis also had similar authority in *binding* and *loosening,* which nor-

mally referred to the imposition or removal of an obligation—including excommunication—through an important doctrinal judgment. This is not meant to suggest that Jesus' practice here can be fully explained in these terms, but it is to note how his own unique torah seems to inform and transform an established Jewish notion already understood in his own day. It must be remembered, however, that most Jews were scandalized when Jesus proclaimed that he, as the Son of man, could forgive sins (cf. Luke 5:20–26).

20:29: "Have you believed because you have seen me? Blessed are those who have not seen and yet have come to believe."
Jesus' pronouncement here on the connection between sight and belief is echoed in other places in Midrash literature. In *Shemoth Rabba* we read: "When the holy blessed God said to Moses, Go, down, for the people have corrupted themselves; he took the tables and would not believe that Israel had sinned saying, 'If I do not see, I will not believe.'" And again in Midrash, *Tillin,* we read: "You, Racha, would you not have believed if you had not seen?" Could Jesus here be evoking such scenes with the great unbelievers? It might seem so, though it is important to note how he puts himself forward as the *object* of the believer's faith—an act unique to Jesus, but presumptive to observant Jews who would reserve such only to God.

6
The Fourth Sunday of Easter, Cycle A
John 10:1–10

Jesus said:
> [10:1]"Amen, amen, I say to you,
> whoever does not enter a sheepfold through the gate
> but climbs over elsewhere is a thief and a robber.
> [2]But whoever enters through the gate is the shepherd of the sheep.
> [3]The gatekeeper opens it for him, and the sheep hear his voice,
> as the shepherd calls his own sheep by name and leads them out.
> [4]When he has driven out all his own,
> he walks ahead of them, and the sheep follow him,
> because they recognize his voice.
> [5]But they will not follow a stranger;
> they will run away from him,
> because they do not recognize the voice of strangers."
> [6]Although Jesus used this figure of speech,
> the Pharisees did not realize what he was trying to tell them.
>
> [7]So Jesus said again, "Amen, amen, I say to you,
> I am the gate for the sheep.
> [8]All who came before me are thieves and robbers,
> but the sheep did not listen to them.
> [9]I am the gate.
> Whoever enters through me will be saved,
> and will come in and go out and find pasture.
> [10]A thief comes only to steal and slaughter and destroy;
> I came so that they might have life and have it more abundantly."

John 10:1–10 presents Jesus as the "gate for the sheep." The image functions by contrasting Jesus' care for the sheep with the intention of others who would steal and slaughter them. The biblical text carries little potential of anti-Judaism because the identity of those who are contrasted to Jesus is not explicit.

However, this benign status is radically altered by the decision of the lectionary to insert the word "Pharisees" into the reading in verse 6 when the Greek literally says "they." The lectionary frequently inserts phrases to help situate and clarify the passages presented. It is difficult to imagine, however, why the insertion of "Pharisees" into this passage was regarded as helpful. Although a case could be made that this passage refers back to Jesus' comments against the Pharisees in chapter 9, an equally credible case can be made that it does not. Even if it is accepted that this passage refers back to the earlier chapter, the reference to the Pharisees is problematic. As will be discussed in the treatment of the man born blind (see Fourth Sunday of Lent, Cycle A), the Pharisees of chapter 9 most likely refer to the Pharisees of the time of the evangelist rather than those of the historical Jesus. Moreover, chapter 9 demonstrates the Johannine tendency of slippage, when it replaces the Pharisees with *hoi Ioudaioi*. (We can only be thankful that the lectionary did not choose to insert "the Jews" into the present selection.)

When these dimensions of the text are appreciated, the insertion of "the Pharisees" into this passage is not only unnecessary but harmful. The literal rendering of the Greek, "*they* did not realize," is just as effective in presenting Jesus as the one who cares for the sheep. When "the Pharisees" are drawn forward from chapter 9 and inserted, the move supports the common misunderstanding that the Pharisees were the primary opponents of the historical Jesus and implies that they are the "thieves and robbers" against whom Jesus rails. Thus the stereotype of the Pharisees as blind, stubborn, and hardened to the needs of others is unfortunately confirmed.

The preacher or catechist who uses this text should be aware of the insertion of "the Pharisees" by the lectionary and be careful not to repeat that designation in the exposition of the passage.

7
Pentecost Sunday, Cycles A, B, C
John 20:19–23

See the Second Sunday of Easter, above.

8
The Third Sunday of Lent, Cycle A
John 4:5–42

⁴ːⁱJesus came to a town of Samaria called Sychar,
    near the plot of land that Jacob had given to his son Joseph.
⁶Jacob's well was there.
Jesus, tired from his journey, sat down there at the well.
It was about noon.

⁷A woman of Samaria came to draw water.
Jesus said to her,
    "Give me a drink."
⁸His disciples had gone into the town to buy food.
⁹The Samaritan woman said to him,
    "How can you, a Jew, ask me, a Samaritan woman, for a drink?"
— For Jews use nothing in common with Samaritans. —
¹⁰Jesus answered and said to her,
    "If you knew the gift of God
    and who is saying to you, 'Give me a drink,'
    you would have asked him
    and he would have given you living water."
¹¹The woman said to him,
    "Sir, you do not even have a bucket and the cistern is deep;
    where then can you get this living water?
¹²Are you greater than our father Jacob,
    who gave us this cistern and drank from it himself
    with his children and his flocks?"
¹³Jesus answered and said to her,
    "Everyone who drinks this water will be thirsty again;
    ¹⁴but whoever drinks the water I shall give will never thirst;
    the water I shall give will become in him
    a spring of water welling up to eternal life."
¹⁵The woman said to him,
    "Sir, give me this water, so that I may not be thirsty
    or have to keep coming here to draw water."

[16]Jesus said to her,

"Go call your husband and come back."

[17]The woman answered and said to him,

"I do not have a husband."

Jesus answered her,

"You are right in saying, 'I do not have a husband.'

[18]For you have had five husbands,

and the one you have now is not your husband.

What you have said is true."

[19]The woman said to him,

"Sir, I can see that you are a prophet.

[20]Our ancestors worshiped on this mountain;

but you people say that the place to worship is in Jerusalem."

[21]Jesus said to her,

"Believe me, woman, the hour is coming

when you will worship the Father

neither on this mountain nor in Jerusalem.

[22]You people worship what you do not understand;

we worship what we understand,

because salvation is from the Jews.

[23]But the hour is coming, and is now here,

when true worshipers will worship the Father in Spirit and truth;

and indeed the Father seeks such people to worship him.

[24]God is Spirit, and those who worship him

must worship in Spirit and truth."

[25]The woman said to him,

"I know that the Messiah is coming, the one called the Christ;

when he comes, he will tell us everything."

[26]Jesus said to her,

"I am he, the one speaking with you."

[27]At that moment his disciples returned,

and were amazed that he was talking with a woman,

but still no one said, "What are you looking for?"

or "Why are you talking with her?"

[28]The woman left her water jar

and went into the town and said to the people,

[29]"Come see a man who told me everything I have done.

Could he possibly be the Christ?"

[30]They went out of the town and came to him.

[31]Meanwhile, the disciples urged him, "Rabbi, eat."

[32]But he said to them,

"I have food to eat of which you do not know."

³³So the disciples said to one another,

   "Could someone have brought him something to eat?"

³⁴Jesus said to them,

   "My food is to do the will of the one who sent me

   and to finish his work.

³⁵Do you not say, 'In four months the harvest will be here'?

I tell you, look up and see the fields ripe for the harvest.

³⁶The reaper is already receiving payment

   and gathering crops for eternal life,

   so that the sower and reaper can rejoice together.

³⁷For here the saying is verified that 'One sows and another reaps.'

³⁸I sent you to reap what you have not worked for;

   others have done the work,

   and you are sharing the fruits of their work."

³⁹Many of the Samaritans of that town began to believe in him

   because of the word of the woman who testified,

   "He told me everything I have done."

⁴⁰When the Samaritans came to him,

   they invited him to stay with them;

   and he stayed there two days.

⁴¹Many more began to believe in him because of his word,

   ⁴²and they said to the woman,

   "We no longer believe because of your word;

   for we have heard for ourselves,

   and we know that this is truly the savior of the world."

Cycle A preserves the ancient tradition of reading the woman at the well, the man born blind, and the raising of Lazarus from John's Gospel on the third, fourth, and fifth Sundays of Lent. This tradition is associated with the preparation of the elect for baptism. These three passages are true highlights of John's Gospel and profoundly moving meditations on faith.

Today's story is a dramatic masterpiece, showing the development within the heart of a nameless Samaritan woman. She is led from suspicion of the stranger she meets at the well (4:9), to the dawning awareness that he possesses marvelous knowledge (4:19), to her active proclamation of his role as Messiah (4:29). Throughout the narrative the Johannine dramatic techniques of misunderstanding (4:11, 15, 33) and irony (4:12) are in full display. The crux of John's Gospel is summed up clearly by Jesus when he indicates the importance of recognizing *who it is* (4:10) who stands before her. The woman must overcome her suspicion, her past life, and her religious perspective to do this, but she succeeds. She becomes a positive example of faith within John's Gospel.

The passage offers opportunities and pitfalls to the preacher or catechist who strives to be sensitive to an anti-Jewish potential within the text. In terms of cautions, one must realize that the origin of this story is most likely connected to the influx of a group of Samaritans who were converted and included into the Johannine community. This makes the story favorable to the Samaritan point of view. The witness of this woman's faith is therefore presented as superior to many of the other Jewish characters who encounter Jesus. Within the Gospel there is an obvious contrast between this scene and the one with Nicodemus which precedes it. Nicodemus, a Jewish leader (3:1), can only muster a perplexed uncertainty in his encounter with Jesus (3:4, 9). The Samaritan woman comes to full and enthusiastic faith.

The preacher should also be careful not to interpret the statement of Jesus in 4:21–24 in a way that rejects the value of Jewish worship. The faith of the Johannine community finds every opportunity to extol the superiority of Jesus over the religious claims of its Jewish neighbors. This section fearlessly claims that true worship will no longer be found in Jerusalem because real worshipers will worship in the Spirit and truth of Jesus. Clearly Christians profess Jesus as the way to the Father, but these verses do not announce an end to Judaism or the validity of its worship. The denigration of Jewish worship found in this passage results at least in part from the need of the Johannine community to react against the practices of the synagogue from which it was expelled.

On the positive side, this passage clearly presents Jesus as a Jew. The Samaritan woman's statement in verse 9 calling Jesus a Jew gives no embarrassment to the evangelist. Moreover, Jesus himself positively asserts that "salvation is from the Jews" (4:22). Certainly this does not negate John's claims of Jesus' superiority. It does show, however, that the Gospel is willing to admit its Jewish roots even after its separation from the synagogue.

This provides an excellent opportunity for the preacher or catechist to emphasize the continuity between the Christian faith and its Jewish origins. Jesus was Jewish, and the salvation he brings flows from the heritage of Judaism. The 1975 Vatican "Guidelines and Suggestions for Implementing the Conciliar Declaration, *Nostra*

Aetate (no. 4)," (section III) reminds us that although Jesus was revealed as the Messiah and Son of God, his gospel was a "fulfillment and perfection" of an earlier revelation. This awareness can be illustrated by citing the words of Jesus to his disciples in 4:34–38. Here Jesus asserts that it is his mission to finish the work of the One who sent him. That "work" includes all that God has been doing throughout Jewish history. The evangelist is not afraid to acknowledge God's true activity in Jewish life and faith before Jesus. Jesus tells the disciples that "others have done the work, and you are sharing the fruits of their work" (4:38). The "others" to whom Jesus refers certainly include Jesus' Jewish ancestors whose faith, sown in time, is now yielding this harvest. Jesus respects the faith of those Jews who have gone before him. It is not by chance, then, that this important scene takes place by the well of the patriarch, Jacob.

Rabbinic Notes on the Samaritan Woman at the Well: John 4:5–42

Readers of the New Testament would do well to consider the relationship between Jesus and Samaritans suggested by the following references in the gospels and the Acts of the Apostles: Luke 17:11; 9:52; 10:33; 17:16; John 4:4ff.; 8:48ff.; Acts 1:8; 8:5ff.; 15:3; 8:25. Each of these stories provides added dimensions to the way in which Christians later understood how the message of Jesus was received by Jews and Samaritans, between whom there were tensions long before the time of Jesus.

Traditionally, Jews have taken their understanding of Samaritans from the historical accounts of 2 Kings 17. Recent discoveries of the Samaritan "Chronicles" that both parallel and diverge from the accounts of Jewish historians like Josephus are now also available.

In any case, the story of the Samaritan woman presents a central problem for the rabbi: how to deal with the relationship of a people whom Jews thought of as no longer fully in covenant with God—a people living apart from mainstream Judaism and accepting only the Torah, but not the prophets. In Samaria was a well precious to both groups: the well where Jacob watered his flocks and tended his sheep (Gen 33:18–20; 43:22; 48:21–22). Joseph was also buried there (Josh 24:32). It was a sacred place and a fine setting in which to demonstrate how the unique torah of Jesus might address non-Jews.

4:7: A Samaritan woman came to draw water, and Jesus said to her, "Give me a drink."

The Samaritan woman approaches the well. For similar scenes of this type, see Genesis 24:11; 29:2 and Exodus 2:15. Jesus is without his followers and asks her, simply: "Give me a drink." By so simple a request, he avoids any real conversation or exchange in accordance with Mishnah *Aboth* 1.5 and Talmud (b) *Berakoth* 43b, which prohibit such between a rabbi and a woman. An additional problem plays in the background for Jesus: Jews considered Samaritan women unclean all the time (cf. Lev 15:19ff as understood in Mishnah, *Niddah* 4.1). Hence, if she were ritually impure, then the bucket she used at the well would also be impure and likewise with the water cup and the water she would offer to Jesus. Surprisingly, Jesus ignores this, even though so many of his teachings and other acts seem allied to many of the Pharisaic schools of thought that would have readily shunned this woman.

4:9: The Samaritan woman said to him, "How is it that you, a Jew, ask a drink of me, a woman of Samaria?"

The woman immediately picks up on Jesus' disregard for the laws of purity and challenges him on both his speaking to a supposedly unclean woman as well as to a *Samaritan woman,* at that.

4:10: Jesus answered her, "If you knew the gift of God, and who it is that is saying to you, 'Give me a drink,' you would have asked him, and he would have given you living water."

Jesus' response to the woman is to make a play on words between "running water"—meaning spring water (found deep in Jacob's well)—and his own torah that, as a form of living teaching, would bring her spiritual refreshment. Jesus may also be alluding to Jeremiah 2:13 or 17:13, where the same image of living water is used. There is also the Palestinian Targum on Genesis 28:10 about the well of Haran: "After our ancestor Jacob had lifted the stone from the mouth of the well, the well rose to its surface and overflowed, and was overflowing twenty years." Indeed, among first-century rabbis, the term "living water" and "the gift of God" are phrases that refer to the Torah directly.

4:12: "Are you greater than our ancestor Jacob...?"

In asking this question, the woman is taking the conversation to its logical and presumptive end. Jesus, in a unique move, responds affirmatively and promises that she, too, could partake of this same kind of water that could flow within her. She then asks him to give her this very water.

4:16: Jesus said to her, "Go, call your husband, and come back."

Jesus' response puzzles the reader but is meant to show a miraculous knowledge. According to Torah, a woman could divorce her husband for several reasons; Jesus simply observes that she has no marriage to speak of. A Jewish reader of the first century, however, would have been shocked by this conversation since the woman, in effect, has revealed—and Jesus has acknowledged—that she is either an adulteress or a mistress. Such an exchange regarding sexual status goes well beyond the bounds of propriety for two strangers, a woman and a man, a Samaritan and a Jew.

4:19–20: The woman said to him, "Sir, I see that you are a prophet. Our ancestors worshiped on this mountain, but you say that the place where people must worship is in Jerusalem."

The woman again tries to steer the conversation her own way by posing a sort of conundrum meant to best the rabbi who had just exposed her own failings. She goes right to the heart of the difference between Samaritans and Jews by asking, in effect, Where is God legitimately and validly worshiped? For Jews, it is in the Temple at Jerusalem; for Samaritans, it is on Mt. Gerezim, their home since 400 BCE.

4:21: Jesus said to her, "Woman, believe me, the hour is coming when you will worship the Father neither on this mountain, nor in Jerusalem."

Jesus' reply is consistent with his own torah: worship is done in neither place—Jerusalem nor Mt. Gerezim—but within the heart, in pursuit of God who pursues us, and in Spirit and truth. This is unique rabbinic teaching in its day and would have been an attractive way for later Judaism in the Diaspora (following the destruction of the Temple) to understand itself as a worshiping community still very much in contact with God. Jesus is also unabashedly Jewish here: Salvation, he says, is from the Jews, not the Samaritans (cf. Ps 76:1). This is followed by his own revelation of himself as the Messiah, or what the Samaritans would have called the "Taheb." It must be remembered that Samaritans did not believe in the Messiah of Judaism, but instead in a kind of "Master Teacher" or prophet. It would seem here that Jesus allowed himself to be understood as this figure. The "Taheb" was to signal God's revelation of the full meaning of the Torah to his people.

4:27: Just then his disciples came. They were astonished that he was speaking with a woman, but no one said, "What do you want?" or "Why are you speaking with her."

It is interesting to note that, as Jesus' disciples return from purchasing food, they immediately raise the same questions of propriety that the Samaritan woman had raised with Jesus at 4:9, suggesting just how striking Jesus' conduct with the woman was in light of Jewish expectations, as well.

4:35: "Do you not say, 'Four months more, then comes the harvest'?"

This sounds very much like a kind of proverb. There are some rabbinical calculations that would verify that there were four months between the sowing and the harvesting of certain crops. The language used at 4:36 may also parallel *Tosefta Peah* 4.18: "My father fathered treasures in this age; I have gathered them in the age to come."

There are perhaps three reflections that would have occurred to a rabbi of the first century upon observing Jesus here. First, he appears thoroughly and completely Jewish in his understanding of much that underlies the story. He loves and appreciates the meaning of Jacob's well, and of the promise of life that would come from torah as "living water"; he views marriage with respect and cannot approve of the serial relationships around which the woman has arranged her life; he defines the Jews as God's instrument of salvation for the whole world—including the Samaritans.

But, secondly, he places concerns for dietary and purity laws— and even for the proprieties of rabbinic behavior with women— below his concern for those whom he finds somehow trapped in their own needs. When Jesus senses a willingness on the part of anyone to explore a "way out" of their quandary, he lays all other considerations aside and reaches out to them in an astonishingly personal way. This was true with Nicodemus, whose inner struggles as a leading Pharisee kept him from talking to Jesus except under the cover of night (John 3:1–21). It is evident later with the woman taken in adultery (John 8:1–12), whom he frees dramatically, not only from the penalties of the law, but perhaps as well from her own sexual behavior. Much of what Jesus does is based on his remarkable intuitive sense as a deeply spiritual person, which is a gift of God and cannot be equated with any school of rabbinic thought or teaching. When he acts in this way, he often represents the best of first-century Jewish life.

Lastly, Jesus puts himself forward in a way that is completely foreign to the expectations even of those who were looking for a Messiah. His tendency to centralize God's saving acts within his own person, his teaching with an authority that often puts him at odds with the Torah of Sinai—these are qualities that must have puzzled and stunned those who watched Jesus, looking for the source of his claims to speak and act as he did.

9
The Fourth Sunday of Lent, Cycle A
John 9:1–41

9:1As Jesus passed by he saw a man blind from birth.
2His disciples asked him,

"Rabbi, who sinned, this man or his parents,
that he was born blind?"

3Jesus answered,

"Neither he nor his parents sinned;
it is so that the works of God might be made visible through him.

4We have to do the works of the one who sent me while it is day.
Night is coming when no one can work.
5While I am in the world, I am the light of the world."
6When he had said this, he spat on the ground

and made clay with the saliva,
and smeared the clay on his eyes,

7and said to him,

"Go wash in the Pool of Siloam" — which means Sent —.
So he went and washed, and came back able to see.

8His neighbors and those who had seen him earlier as a beggar said,

"Isn't this the one who used to sit and beg?"

9Some said, "It is, "

but others said, "No, he just looks like him."

He said, "I am."
10So they said to him, "How were your eyes opened?"
11He replied,

"The man called Jesus made clay and anointed my eyes
and told me, 'Go to Siloam and wash.'

So I went there and washed and was able to see."
12And they said to him, "Where is he?"
He said, "I don't know."

13They brought the one who was once blind to the Pharisees.
14Now Jesus had made clay and opened his eyes on a sabbath.

¹⁵So then the Pharisees also asked him how he was able to see.
He said to them,
    "He put clay on my eyes, and I washed, and now I can see."
¹⁶So some of the Pharisees said,
    "This man is not from God,
    because he does not keep the sabbath."
But others said,
    "How can a sinful man do such signs?"
And there was a division among them.
¹⁷So they said to the blind man again,
    "What do you have to say about him,
    since he opened your eyes?"
He said, "He is a prophet."

¹⁸Now the Jews did not believe
    that he had been blind and gained his sight
    until they summoned the parents of the one who had gained his sight.
¹⁹They asked them,
    "Is this your son, who you say was born blind?
How does he now see?"
²⁰His parents answered and said,
    "We know that this is our son and that he was born blind.
²¹We do not know how he sees now,
    nor do we know who opened his eyes.
Ask him, he is of age;
    he can speak for himself."
²²His parents said this because they were afraid
    of the Jews, for the Jews had already agreed
    that if anyone acknowledged him as the Christ,
    he would be expelled from the synagogue.
²³For this reason his parents said,
    "He is of age; question him."

²⁴So a second time they called the man who had been blind
    and said to him, "Give God the praise!
We know that this man is a sinner."
²⁵He replied,
    "If he is a sinner, I do not know.
One thing I do know is that I was blind and now I see."
²⁶So they said to him,
    "What did he do to you?
    How did he open your eyes?"
²⁷He answered them,
    "I told you already and you did not listen.
Why do you want to hear it again?

Do you want to become his disciples, too?"
[28]They ridiculed him and said,

"You are that man's disciple;
we are disciples of Moses!
[29]We know that God spoke to Moses,
but we do not know where this one is from."
[30]The man answered and said to them,

"This is what is so amazing,
that you do not know where he is from, yet he opened my eyes.
[31]We know that God does not listen to sinners,
but if one is devout and does his will, he listens to him.
[32]It is unheard of that anyone ever opened the eyes of a person born blind.
[33]If this man were not from God,
he would not be able to do anything."
[34]They answered and said to him,

"You were born totally in sin,
and are you trying to teach us?"
Then they threw him out.

[35]When Jesus heard that they had thrown him out,
he found him and said, "Do you believe in the Son of Man?"
[36]He answered and said,

"Who is he, sir, that I may believe in him?"
[37]Jesus said to him,

"You have seen him,
and the one speaking with you is he."
[38]He said,

"I do believe, Lord," and he worshiped him.
[39]Then Jesus said,

"I came into this world for judgment,
so that those who do not see might see,
and those who do see might become blind."

[40]Some of the Pharisees who were with him heard this
and said to him, "Surely we are not also blind, are we?"
[41]Jesus said to them,

"If you were blind, you would have no sin;
but now you are saying, 'We see,' so your sin remains."

One can argue that this passage is the most powerful conversion story in the New Testament. Beginning with an act of healing, John has extended the narration in such a way that we are witnesses to a maturing of faith in Christ. The man who had been blind from birth grows throughout the story. At first he only knows that it was Jesus who healed him (9:9–12). Gradually he recognizes Jesus as a prophet (9:17), as one from God (9:33), and finally as the Son of man to be worshiped (9:35–38). The man born blind does not come to this recognition without opposition. But the more he is challenged, the more he stands his ground insisting that he was blind but now he sees (9:25). The story is both compelling and beautiful, asserting that the power of faith can flourish even in the midst of hostility.

The problem of anti-Jewish bias is centered in the way the hostility toward Jesus and the man born blind is expressed. At the beginning (9:13, 15, 16) and at the end (9:40) of the story, it is the Pharisees who are identified as the opponents. In the center of the story, however, it is *hoi Ioudaioi* (often translated as "the Jews"). This should not surprise us. As we discussed in the Introduction, *hoi Ioudaioi* has the tendency in John's Gospel to replace other terms for Jesus' opponents. That *hoi Ioudaioi* does not refer to all Jews in this story is quite clear. The man born blind, his parents, and Jesus himself are all Jewish! The sensitive preacher or catechist will recognize that *hoi Ioudaioi,* in this story, is a technical Johannine word referring to "some of the religious leaders."

Furthermore, the interpreter should remember that the decision to expel the followers of Jesus from the synagogue (9:22) is not to be located in the time of the historical Jesus. It reflects the experience of the Johannine community toward the end of the first century CE. The authorities attack the man born blind in 9:28–29, "You are that man's disciple; we are disciples of Moses! We know that God spoke to Moses, but we do not know where this one is from." These assertions can be seen to reflect the complaints of the synagogue leaders against the Johannine community. The sudden shift to "we" in the response of the man born blind (9:31) may well be intended to indicate how John's community responded to such complaints.

The interpreter should read the presence of "the Pharisees" in this story in light of the history of the Johannine community. Because the Pharisees emerged as the primary Jewish group after the destruction of the Temple, the Gospel is inclined to show the Pharisees as Jesus' primary opponents. It is unwarranted, however, to suppose that the Pharisees presented a united front against the historical Jesus. The story itself affirms this viewpoint when it tells us that the Pharisees were divided over Jesus' identity (9:16–17). However, as the narration proceeds, "the Pharisees" are nevertheless presented as an undifferentiated group. The preacher or catechist should therefore appreciate that when the text speaks of "the Pharisees," it is referring to "some of the Pharisees," or even more precisely "some of the religious leaders."

In typical Johannine style all characters in the story side either for or against Jesus. Those who believe are able to see spiritually. Those who do not believe are spiritually blind. The story plays artistically with the difference between physical and spiritual sight: "If you were blind, you would have no sin; but now you are saying, 'We see,' so your sin remains" (9:41). This "sin" to which the text refers is, of course, the failure to believe in Jesus. As the preacher or catechist lifts up the central importance of faith in Jesus throughout this story, care must be taken in identifying who it is that fails to believe. It is misleading to give the impression that those in blindness were simply "the Jews" or "the Pharisees." For there were certainly some Jews and most probably some Pharisees who did believe.

Despite John's tendency to relegate "the Pharisees" and *hoi Ioudaioi* to the negative side of his cosmic dualism, this text does not require us to view Jews today or their ancestors as "spiritually blind" or "in sin." Responsible preaching and catechesis will make it clear that such false conclusions cannot be based upon the authority of the scriptures.

Rabbinic Notes on the Cure of the Man Born Blind: John 9:1–41

This story poses a question central to rabbinic discussion of Jesus' day: Is illness God's punishment for sin? Throughout this story, the relationship of the sinner to God, of illness to sin, and of sin to punishment is explored from several points of view. Jesus' teaching denies that the disability of the blind man came from his sin or that of his parents. Instead, this blindness is one whose cure signals the arrival of messianic times. Just as Jesus connects sin and self-deception in John 9:41, so he connects sin and divine punishment in John 5:14. This was a rabbinic practice emanating from commonplace readings of the scriptures (Exod 20:5, Ezek 18:20, Exod 4:11, Deut 28:28).

9:2: His disciples asked him, "Rabbi, who sinned, this man or his parents, that he was born blind ?"

The way the question is put to Jesus is in its most natural and conversational form (cf. also Luke 13:2). Some rabbis thought that an infant could sin in the womb (cf. Exod 20:5).

9:5: As long as I am in the world, I am the light of the world.

"I am" here would have been taken as a messianic signal, found in other passages—John 4:25ff.; 8:24, 28, 58; 13:19; 18:5, 6, 8—and developed from Deuteronomy 26:5ff., where "I am" is used to denote the presence of the redeeming God at that moment in Jewish history (cf. *Haggadah* prayers at Seder). See also Isaiah 35:5 and 42:7 for a messianic cure of blindness, as well as the Midrash on Psalm 146:8. Some rabbis thought that in the messianic times to come that neither fault nor merit would pass from one generation to another, but each would be accountable solely for its own deeds.

9:6: When he had said this, he spat on the ground and made mud with the saliva and spread the mud on the man's eyes.

The Talmud is filled with various therapies for the cure of many different blindnesses in the ancient world (cf.Talmud, *Tosefta Shabbath* in 105a, in opposition to Rashi). Spittle of prominent persons was considered especially healing (Rashi, on Numbers 3:12, and *Baba Bathra* 126b, especially regarding the saliva of the firstborn son). A paste created with spittle and wheat flour was a very common remedy (cf.Talmud, *Hullin* 11:1b). Jesus' special clay spittle mixture was done at least to show that he was not using charms or magic, but was following the practice of his day. However, he is faulted thereby in breaking the Sabbath laws in three ways: (1) mixing clay with spittle was prohibited as a part of the law of observance of the holiness of the Sabbath (Mishnah, *Shabbath* 7.2.39); (2) in Talmud, *Bab Abodah Zorah* 28b, Sabbath anointings for the eyes are forbidden explicitly, and (3) since a man's life was not at stake on the Sabbath, then his cure—like that of anyone with a long-standing condition—could wait until the following day.

9:7: [Jesus said to him,] "Go, wash in the Pool of Siloam" (which means Sent). Then he went and washed and came back able to see.

Not unlike Naaman and others before him, the blind man is put to the test of faith: to trust the prophet Elijah—or, in this case, Jesus—to go and wash (cf. 2 Kgs 5:10–14).

9:18, 21–23: They called the parents of the man who had received his sight…. "Ask him; he is of age; he will speak for himself." His parents said this because they were afraid of the Jews; for the Jews had already agreed that anyone who confessed Jesus to be the Messiah would be put out of the synagogue. Therefore his parents said, "He is of age; ask him."

Surely this passage, more than any other in the story, carries with it the possibility of an anti-Jewish reading. When the man born blind is questioned, a legal formula is used in order to guarantee that his answer will be taken under a quasi-juridical investigative form by the Pharisees (cf. Josh 7:19 and 1 Esdras 9:8–9), suggesting that many were already suspicious of the miracles of Jesus. Blind persons who did not witness an act could not be called to testify in regard to it (cf. Maimonides, *Hilchoth Eduth* 9.12, *Baba Bathra* 128a, and Tosefta, *Sanhedrin* 5.4), so the parents of the blind man, as the most authoritative witnesses of his condition, would be called to give testimony. As for expulsion from the synagogue (cf. John 12:42 and 16:2), most scholars agree that this is an interpolation of the text, later projected back into this particular story, since expulsion from the synagogues for Christians was not recorded until closer to 80 CE.

10
The Fifth Sunday of Lent, Cycle A
John 11:1–45

11:1Now a man was ill, Lazarus from Bethany,
   the village of Mary and her sister Martha.
2Mary was the one who had anointed the Lord with perfumed oil
   and dried his feet with her hair;
   it was her brother Lazarus who was ill.
3So the sisters sent word to Jesus saying,
   "Master, the one you love is ill."
4When Jesus heard this he said,
   "This illness is not to end in death,
   but is for the glory of God,
   that the Son of God may be glorified through it."
5Now Jesus loved Martha and her sister and Lazarus.
6So when he heard that he was ill,
   he remained for two days in the place where he was.
7Then after this he said to his disciples,
   "Let us go back to Judea."
8The disciples said to him,
   "Rabbi, the Jews were just trying to stone you,
   and you want to go back there?"
9Jesus answered,
   "Are there not twelve hours in a day?
If one walks during the day, he does not stumble,
   because he sees the light of this world.
10But if one walks at night, he stumbles,
   because the light is not in him."
11He said this, and then told them,
   "Our friend Lazarus is asleep,
   but I am going to awaken him."
12So the disciples said to him,
   "Master, if he is asleep, he will be saved."
13But Jesus was talking about his death,
   while they thought that he meant ordinary sleep.

¹⁴So then Jesus said to them clearly,
    "Lazarus has died.
¹⁵And I am glad for you that I was not there,
    that you may believe.
Let us go to him."
¹⁶So Thomas, called Didymus, said to his fellow disciples,
    "Let us also go to die with him."

¹⁷When Jesus arrived, he found that Lazarus
    had already been in the tomb for four days.
¹⁸Now Bethany was near Jerusalem, only about two miles away.
¹⁹And many of the Jews had come to Martha and Mary
    to comfort them about their brother.
²⁰When Martha heard that Jesus was coming,
    she went to meet him;
    but Mary sat at home.
²¹Martha said to Jesus,
    "Lord, if you had been here,
    my brother would not have died.
²²But even now I know that whatever you ask of God,
    God will give you."
²³Jesus said to her,
    "Your brother will rise."
²⁴Martha said to him,
    "I know he will rise,
    in the resurrection on the last day."
²⁵Jesus told her,
    "I am the resurrection and the life;
    whoever believes in me, even if he dies, will live,
    ²⁶and everyone who lives and believes in me will never die.
Do you believe this?"
²⁷She said to him, "Yes, Lord.
I have come to believe that you are the Christ, the Son of God,
    the one who is coming into the world."

²⁸When she had said this,
    she went and called her sister Mary secretly, saying,
    "The teacher is here and is asking for you."
²⁹As soon as she heard this,
    she rose quickly and went to him.
³⁰For Jesus had not yet come into the village,
    but was still where Martha had met him.
³¹So when the Jews who were with her in the house comforting her
    saw Mary get up quickly and go out,

they followed her,
     presuming that she was going to the tomb to weep there.
[32]When Mary came to where Jesus was and saw him,
     she fell at his feet and said to him,
     "Lord, if you had been here,
     my brother would not have died."
[33]When Jesus saw her weeping and the Jews who had come with her
          weeping,
     he became perturbed and deeply troubled, [34]and said,
     "Where have you laid him?"
They said to him, "Sir, come and see."
[35]And Jesus wept.
[36]So the Jews said, "See how he loved him."
[37]But some of them said,
     "Could not the one who opened the eyes of the blind man
     have done something so that this man would not have died?"

[38]So Jesus, perturbed again, came to the tomb.
It was a cave, and a stone lay across it.
[39]Jesus said, "Take away the stone."
Martha, the dead man's sister, said to him,
     "Lord, by now there will be a stench;
     he has been dead for four days."
[40]Jesus said to her,
     "Did I not tell you that if you believe
     you will see the glory of God?"
[41]So they took away the stone.
And Jesus raised his eyes and said,
     "Father, I thank you for hearing me.
[42]I know that you always hear me;
     but because of the crowd here I have said this,
     that they may believe that you sent me."
[43]And when he had said this,
     he cried out in a loud voice,
     "Lazarus, come out!"
[44]The dead man came out,
     tied hand and foot with burial bands,
     and his face was wrapped in a cloth.
So Jesus said to them,
     "Untie him and let him go."

[45]Now many of the Jews who had come to Mary
     and seen what he had done began to believe in him.

This story of the raising of Lazarus contains one of the highest expressions of Johannine faith. Martha is able to profess Jesus as the resurrection and the life, the Messiah, the Son of God, the one who is coming into the world and the one through whom those who believe will never die (11:25–27). The raising of Lazarus, who has been in the tomb for four days, is the visible sign that testifies to this faith. It is the climactic sign of Jesus' ministry. John has the tendency of moving the opposition against Jesus into earlier phases of his ministry (see Introduction). Therefore, John uses this greatest of Jesus' signs as the occasion when Jesus' opponents decide to seek his death (11:46–53).

Early in the Lazarus story there is reference to the danger Jesus should expect in Judea. When Jesus announces that he will go to Lazarus, the disciples object that he was just in Judea and was almost stoned there (11:7–8). It is likely that these verses are an addition by the evangelist to tie the story of Lazarus more closely to the theme of Jesus' death. The mention of stoning refers back to earlier scenes within the Gospel (8:59; 10:31). Because of John's inclination to project the opposition to Jesus back into earlier sections of his narrative, one need not conclude that such attacks against the historical Jesus took place before his final days in Jerusalem.

What makes the disciples' comment in verses 7–8 potentially dangerous is that it identifies those trying to kill Jesus as *hoi Ioudaioi*. The reader will remember these verses have led some commentators to argue that *hoi Ioudaioi* should be translated "the Judeans" (see Introduction). Most translations, however, render the phrase as "the Jews" (as in the lectionary). This could well give the impression that there was a desire on the part of the whole Jewish people to kill Jesus. The informed reader will recognize that *hoi Ioudaioi* in this verse refers to "the Temple authorities" who were aligned with Pilate to keep the Roman peace. Preachers and catechists will seek ways to promote such an accurate understanding of *hoi Ioudaioi* within these verses.

The story itself can be used in this clarification, for it contains five instances in which *hoi Ioudaioi* is used in a positive sense. In 11:19, 31 *hoi Ioudaioi* are the friends of Martha and Mary who come to console them. In 11:33 they weep with Mary and cause Jesus to weep as well. In 11:36 they recognize in Jesus' tears his closeness to Lazarus and remark, "See how he loved him." In 11:45 we are told that many of *hoi Ioudaioi* believed in Jesus. Depending on how closely one chooses to tie the modifying clause in Greek, it is possible to understand that those who believed were all of those who came to grieve with Martha and Mary. *Hoi Ioudaioi* in all these cases refers to Jews who are sympathetic and believers. This should remind the interpreter of this passage that *hoi Ioudaioi* in 11:8 cannot be understood to claim that "all the Jews" sought to kill Jesus.

Since *hoi Ioudaioi* is so frequently presented within the Gospel in the polemical sense, the preacher or catechist would be wise to seize on this opportunity to stress its more positive usage. Emphasizing the love, sympathy, and faith of the Jewish friends of Martha and Mary will place a positive impression of Jews within the imaginations of those who hear this story. This will make it clear that even in John "the Jews" cannot be colored in wholly negative terms.

11
Trinity Sunday, Cycle A
John 3:16–18

This is a shorter version of John 3:14–21. Refer to the Fourth Sunday of Lent, Cycle B, below.

12
The Most Holy Body and Blood of Christ (Corpus Christi), Cycle A
John 6:51–58

The gospel selection for the feast of The Most Holy Body and Blood of Christ in Cycle A is the same passage chosen for the Twentieth Sunday of the Year in Cycle B (see below). There is, however, one peculiar variation. In Cycle B the lectionary, as it frequently does, adds a line to introduce the scene: "Jesus said to the crowds." Here on the feast of Corpus Christi the lectionary introduces the same passage with the words, "Jesus said to the Jewish crowds." The passage includes a polemical use of *hoi Ioudaioi* in 6:52, giving the impression that "all Jews" not just "some in the crowd" are disputing with Jesus. Therefore, to highlight the Jewish nature of the crowd in the introductory line is both unnecessary and misleading. It complicates the task of the preacher or catechist to clarify that it was the lack of faith in the crowd, not its Jewish nature, that proved detrimental. The scene-setting phrase in Cycle B, "Jesus said to the crowds," is to be preferred.

Readings from the Gospel of John in Cycle B

13
The Third Sunday of Advent, Cycle B
John 1:6–8, 19–28

^{1:6}A man named John was sent from God.
⁷He came for testimony, to testify to the light,
 so that all might believe through him.
⁸He was not the light,
 but came to testify to the light.

¹⁹And this is the testimony of John.
When the Jews from Jerusalem sent priests
 and Levites to him
 to ask him, "Who are you?"
 ²⁰He admitted and did not deny it,
 but admitted, "I am not the Christ."
²¹So they asked him,
 "What are you then? Are you Elijah?"
And he said, "I am not."
"Are you the Prophet?"
He answered, "No."
²²So they said to him,
 "Who are you, so we can give an answer to those who sent us?
What do you have to say for yourself?"
²³He said:
 "I am *the voice of one crying out in the desert,*
 "make straight the way of the Lord,"
 as Isaiah the prophet said."
²⁴Some Pharisees were also sent.
²⁵They asked him,
 "Why then do you baptize
 if you are not the Christ or Elijah or the Prophet?"
²⁶John answered them,
 "I baptize with water;
 but there is one among you whom you do not recognize,
 ²⁷the one who is coming after me,

whose sandal strap I am not worthy to untie."
²⁸This happened in Bethany across the Jordan,
     where John was baptizing.

The lectionary selection for this Sunday draws together two passages concerning John the Baptist. Verses 6–8 have been extracted from John's prologue to serve as an introduction to the questioning of the Baptizer that follows (1:19–28). This second section provides an excellent example of the complex manner in which the Gospel of John identifies opponents (see Introduction).

In verse 19 we are told that *hoi Ioudaioi* sent priests and Levites to question John. Although *hoi Ioudaioi* is usually translated "the Jews," it makes little sense to understand the term as referring to all Jews. It would be impossible for all Jews to send a delegation that was itself composed of Jews. *Hoi Ioudaioi* must refer in this verse, as it often does, to a subset within Judaism—probably the authorities in Jerusalem hostile to Jesus. However, in verse 24 another difficulty emerges. There we are told that those who were sent were from the Pharisees. The expression in Greek is ambiguous. Does "those who were sent" in verse 24 refer to "the priests and Levites" of verse 19? If that is the case, then the passage sees the Pharisees and *hoi Ioudaioi* as the same group. The New Revised Standard Version opts for this understanding by translating, "Now they had been sent from the Pharisees." But the situation is difficult to accept historically. The Pharisees at the time of Jesus would not have been in a position of authority to send a delegation of priests and Levites (who were Sadducees) to question John the Baptist.

It is, however, possible that the evangelist, writing after the destruction of the Temple when the Pharisees were the prominent Jewish group, conflated the Pharisees with the Temple authorities and felt free to use "the Pharisees" and *hoi Ioudaioi* interchangeably. Consistency in naming opposition groups is not the hallmark of this Gospel. As we discussed in the Introduction, the evangelist seems to allow the terminology which identifies Jesus' opponents to fluctuate. He demonstrates the same freedom in naming the opponents of the Baptist. Writing as the evangelist did at the end of the first century and already separated from the synagogue, distinctions between Jewish religious groups did not overly concern him.

Another possibility is to read verse 24 as introducing a new group—this time a group of Pharisees. The lectionary translation adopts this view by translating, "Some Pharisees were also sent." The "also" is not in the Greek text but has been included in the translation to suggest this particular understanding. This translation has the advantage of recognizing the historical difficulty of conflating the Pharisees with the earlier-mentioned priests and Levites.

The preacher or catechist should be aware of the ambiguity in this verse concerning the identity of those who question the Baptist. Nuance should be introduced into any discussion of those who were interrogating the Baptist and what their intentions were. The evangelist is capable of using the all-encompassing term, *hoi Ioudaioi*, to tag those who oppose Jesus and the Baptist. Caution should guide any conclusions concerning the historical accuracy of the disagreements between Jesus or the Baptist and those who are identified as their opponents. I do not suggest that the preacher exhaust the assembly with all the intricacies of translation. I do, however, encourage the preacher to be aware of the ambiguity in the text and to adopt in preaching an equally ambiguous phrase such as "the religious leaders" to identify those who question the Baptist.

14
The Third Sunday of Lent, Cycle B
John 2:13–25

2:13Since the Passover of the Jews was near,
  Jesus went up to Jerusalem.
14He found in the temple area those who sold oxen, sheep, and doves,
  as well as the money changers seated there.
15He made a whip out of cords
  and drove them all out of the temple area, with the sheep and oxen,
  and spilled the coins of the money changers
  and overturned their tables,
16and to those who sold doves he said,
  "Take these out of here,
  and stop making my Father's house a marketplace."
17His disciples recalled the words of Scripture,
  Zeal for your house will consume me.
18At this the Jews answered and said to him,
  "What sign can you show us for doing this?"
19Jesus answered and said to them,
  "Destroy this temple and in three days I will raise it up."
20The Jews said,
  "This temple has been under construction for forty-six years,
  and you will raise it up in three days?"
21But he was speaking about the temple of his body.
22Therefore, when he was raised from the dead,
  his disciples remembered that he had said this,
  and they came to believe the Scripture
  and the word Jesus had spoken.

23While he was in Jerusalem for the feast of Passover,
  many began to believe in his name
  when they saw the signs he was doing.
24But Jesus would not trust himself to them because he knew them all,
    25and did not need anyone to testify about human nature.
He himself understood it well.

The gospel for this Sunday is John's version of Jesus' action in the Temple. This is one of the few scenes John shares with the Synoptic gospels. In interpreting this passage, it is important not to merge the details from the various gospel accounts or to blur the difference between this incident during the ministry of the historical Jesus (stage one of the gospel tradition) and its interpretation by the evangelist (stage three). Let us, then, first examine John's account in comparison to the other evangelists (stage three) and then address its relation to stage one.

Unlike the Synoptic gospels, which present Jesus' action in the Temple shortly before his passion, John recounts the scene at the beginning of his ministry during the first of three journeys to Jerusalem to celebrate the feast of Passover. This does not, however, indicate a desire to disassociate Jesus' action in the Temple from his passion and glorification. Quite the contrary. This action on his first trip to celebrate Passover is meant to emphasize the suffering and exaltation that will occur during his third Passover trip. The evangelist achieves this emphasis by including two additions that are not present in the Synoptic accounts. In 2:17 the disciples upon seeing Jesus' action remember the passage from Psalm 69:9, "It is zeal for your house that has consumed me." John, however, has changed the tense of the verb: "Zeal for your house *will* consume me." By this alteration the evangelist is linking Jesus' action in the Temple to his future death.

The second addition is Jesus' answer to those who question his authority for acting as he did in the Temple. In the Synoptic accounts Jesus responds by posing a question concerning John the Baptist. In John's Gospel Jesus responds by saying, "Destroy this temple, and in three days I will raise it up" (2:19). Two verses later the narrator of the Gospel explains that Jesus was referring to the temple of his body. Therefore, John so shapes Jesus' action in the Temple that it not only points to Jesus' passion but also to his glorification. For the Johannine community true worship is no longer to be found in the Temple. Indeed, at the time of the writing of John's Gospel the Jerusalem Temple had been in ruins for more than twenty years. For John it is Jesus in his own person who is now the way to genuine worship.

Let us now ask what connection this scene has to Jesus' historical ministry in stage one? Jesus' action in the Temple is so often called "the cleansing of the Temple" that readers seldom stop to question why cleansing would be needed. The idea of cleansing doubtlessly arises because Jesus speaks of a "den of robbers" (Mark 11:17) or "a marketplace" (John 2:16). When we ask, however, what might have been the cause of robbery or improper trade that required "cleansing," there is no simple response. It is dubious to presume that the historical Jesus was opposed to Temple worship or animal sacrifice. Such attitudes, while perfectly understandable to modern sensibilities, would make little sense to a Jew of the first century. Jesus was such a Jew, and there are several passages in the New Testament that attest to his respect for the Temple. Neither is it convincing to suggest that Jesus was opposed to the selling of animals in the Temple. Such a view would also betray a lack of appreciation for Jewish sacrificial worship. Sacrifices necessitate a suitable supply of animals and the proper monetary arrangements to purchase them.

We come closer to probability with the suggestion that Jesus was opposed to the *way* in which these necessary aspects of Temple worship were carried out. Perhaps Jesus was opposed to those who exchanged money unfairly or to the manner in which the priests performed their duties. Perhaps. Yet outside of this story there is very little complaint to be found in the gospels concerning the running of the Temple or the suitability of its priests.

Because of the difficulty in identifying the cause that motivated Jesus to "cleanse" the Temple, it is better to understand Jesus' action from another perspective. It could have been intended as a symbolic action, similar to those performed by the prophets. E. P. Sanders (*Jesus and Judaism,* 61–76) has argued that the symbolism of Jesus' action pointed to the arrival of the messianic age. In that age God was expected to destroy the present Temple and provide a new temple from heaven. Therefore, when the historical Jesus turned over some tables of the money changers in the Temple, he may have intended his action to be seen as a prophetic sign that such an eschatological event was soon to appear. This interpretation has the advantage of tying Jesus' action in the Temple to a theme that we are quite certain was central to his historical ministry: the announcement of the imminent reign of God. If Sanders is correct, it is possible to understand Jesus' action in stage one of the gospel tradition not as a criticism of the Jewish Temple or its functioning, but rather as a symbolic announcement that the reign of God was at hand.

As the preacher or catechist approaches this passage, it is important to keep the stages of the gospel tradition and the difficulties in interpreting those stages in mind. If the choice is to highlight John's emphasis on the passion and glorification, this good news should not be presented against some presumed background of a corrupt Temple. If one would prefer to emphasize the need of cleansing and reform (which can certainly be derived from 2:16), reasons that are historically improbable should be avoided. It is difficult to ascribe either an opposition to Temple worship or the selling of animals for Temple sacrifice to the Jewish Jesus of stage one. If one opts to center on Jesus' desire to reform supposed abuses in the Temple, it is only fair to admit that such possible abuses did not characterize all those who functioned in the Temple and that similar abuses can be found among every religious group, including our own.

If the preacher or catechist would choose to present Jesus' action not as a cleansing but as a prophetic sign, then the way is open to connect the historical Jesus both to his past and to our future. Jesus would then stand in the ancient tradition of the Jewish prophets who spoke for God and in the long line of Jewish believers who awaited the messianic age. Jesus would also, by his action, point to those future events that his followers came to see as the fulfillment of that messianic promise: his dying and rising. This option avoids the presumption of abuse in the Temple, which is historically dubious. It also highlights the passion and glorification of Jesus that are clearly John's theological concern.

Informed preachers and catechists will also recognize in this passage the presence of John's polemical use of *hoi Ioudaioi* (see Introduction). The term occurs three times (2:13, 18, 20). In 2:18 and 20 *hoi Ioudaioi* are clearly Jesus' opponents, although they are not particularly hostile ones. As is typical of the Johannine use, these opponents cannot be equated with all the Jews, even though the translation, "the Jews," would tend to give that impression. When we examine the Synoptic versions of Jesus' action in the Temple and the debates that follow it (Mark 11:27–28; Matt 21:23; Luke 20:1–2), those who question Jesus' authority are the chief priests and the elders. (Mark and Luke include the scribes as well.) This makes historical sense since it would have been the chief priests and elders who controlled the Temple and who would be most disturbed by Jesus' action. Therefore, it seems likely that John's *hoi Ioudaioi* in verses 18 and 20 have the Temple authorities as their true referent.

The use of *hoi Ioudaioi* in 2:13 does not seem polemical. It is, however, unnecessary. To speak of "the Passover of the Jews" begs the question of "who else's Passover might it be?" What we see here, of course, is the perspective of the Johannine community writing at a later time when the separation from the synagogue and perhaps from the Jewish feasts was complete. The implication is that the Passover was "their feast" and "no longer ours." What is clearly anachronistic about this viewpoint is that although it might have no longer been the feast of the Johannine community, it was certainly the feast of the historical Jesus. Jesus celebrated the Passover as a Jew. This truth will not be overlooked in accurate preaching and teaching.

Rabbinic Notes on the Money Changers in the Temple: John 2:13–25

In this story (cf. Matt 21:12ff., Mark 11:15, and Luke 19:45) John presents an important and recurrent theme of many of his stories: the relationship of Jesus to the Temple. No fewer than nine separate stores in John link Jesus to the Temple in some way (cf. John 2:13ff.; 5:14; 7:14; 7:28; 8:2, 20, 59; 10:23; 11:56). One of these—John 8:20 (cf. Mark 12:41ff.)—demonstrates the importance of Jesus' preaching at the site of the Temple treasury in particular. In all such stories, Jesus shows a heightened sense of the Temple as *the* place on earth beyond all others where God dwells with his people.

2:13: The Passover of the Jews was near, and Jesus went up to Jerusalem.
Here, Jesus is portrayed as an observant Jew, preparing himself to enter into the annual cycle of sacrifice and prayer held in Jerusalem in honor of the Passover. It is against the background of fidelity to his Jewish heritage that his encounter with money changers and sellers is to be understood.

2:14: In the temple he found people selling cattle, sheep, and doves, and the money changers seated at their tables.
Where in the "temple area" could these men have been located? Most likely it was in the Court of the Gentiles, which surrounded the inner barrier leading to the courts of women, men, and, finally, of the priests, where sacrifices were offered (see Josephus, *Wars*, 5.5.1–6). In the Court of Gentiles, for example, sheep and doves (as the offering of the poor) were sold, while a special tax was collected annually on every Jewish male over nineteen years of age (Exod 30:11–16, Neh 10:33) for the upkeep of the Temple itself. Such

monies—a half-shekel—supplied funds for the endless sacrifices of oxen and incense within the Temple. The "money changers" referred to by John were private individuals whose task it was to convert Roman coins into the special "Tyrian shekel," or official coinage of the Temple economy. The role of these workers or "shul-hani" is laid out in Tosefta, *Shekalim* 2.13; they were allowed to charge a 4 percent or greater fee for every coin exchange they made (Tosefta, *Shekalim* 1.6ff.). Many of these same workers also accepted money for investment and paid out interest on it as a loan, in violation of Jewish law (cf. Deut 23:20–21, Exod 23:24, and Lev 25:35–38).

2:15–16: Making a whip of cords, he drove all of them out of the temple, both the sheep and the cattle. He also poured out the coins of the money changers and overturned their tables. He told those who were selling doves, "Take these things out of here! Stop making my Father's house a marketplace."

Here, Jesus addresses what is presumably a series of abuses against money lending noted above, and shows himself as a defender of Temple purity in the mode of Zechariah, the fiery sixth-century BCE prophet, whose message was the joyful expectation of the rebuilding of the Temple in messianic times. Jesus' statement in v. 16 parallels Zechariah 14:21: "And there should no longer be traders in the house of the LORD of hosts on that day."

2:20: The Jews then said, "This temple has been under construction for forty-six years, and will you raise it up in three days?"

The question refers to the forty-six years taken to build the second or Herodian Temple, begun by King Herod in c. 22 BCE (cf. Josephus, *Antiquities,* 15,11,1,380). Jesus' use of the term "three days" could be intended as a reference to the voice of the prophet Hosea 6:2: "After two days he will revive us; on the third day he will raise us up that we may live before him." Such a time sequence— "after two days; on the third day"—reflects Jewish belief in the irreversibility of death following the third day after expiration. A parallel can be found in John's account of the death and raising of Lazarus (John 11:1–48), in which Martha, the sister of Lazarus and friend of Jesus, remarks aloud at the grave site: "Lord, already there is a stench because he has been dead four days" (11:39).

15
The Fourth Sunday of Lent, Cycle B
John 3:14–21

Jesus said to Nicodemus: ·
   ³:¹⁴"Just as Moses lifted up the serpent in the desert,
   so must the Son of Man be lifted up,
   ¹⁵so that everyone who believes in him may have eternal life."

¹⁶For God so loved the world that he gave his only Son,
   so that everyone who believes in him might not perish
   but might have eternal life.
¹⁷For God did not send his Son into the world to condemn the world,
   but that the world might be saved through him.
¹⁸Whoever believes in him will not be condemned,
   but whoever does not believe has already been condemned,
   because he has not believed in the name of the only Son of God.
¹⁹And this is the verdict,
   that the light came into the world,
   but people preferred darkness to light,
   because their works were evil.
²⁰For everyone who does wicked things hates the light
   and does not come toward the light,
   so that his works might not be exposed.
²¹But whoever lives the truth comes to the light,
   so that his works may be clearly seen as done in God.

    This is one of the most popular passages in the New Testament. It provides a beautiful expression of the good news: "God so loved the world that he gave his only Son" (3:16). As we read on, however, an accompanying note of condemnation is also sounded: "...whoever does not believe has already been condemned, because he has not believed in the name of the only Son of God" (3:18). Clearly John's exclusive dualism is at work in this passage (see Introduction). The stark contrast between light and darkness in the concluding verses only confirms the perspective that is present from the beginning. If those who believe in Christ are by that decision "saved," then those who do not believe are by that decision "condemned." This contrast illustrates the manner in which John envisions judgment as already present in the decision of the believer or nonbeliever.

There is no explicit mention in this passage of Jews who do not accept the gospel of Christ. Rather all those who do not accept the high Christology of John are grouped together on the negative side of John's dualism. Christians who hear this passage will not spontaneously conclude that Jews are condemned, but Jews who hear this passage may easily understand that it claims they are cut off from God.

Because John draws his options in stark alternatives, there seems to be no room left for Jews who, in good conscience, do not accept Jesus as the way to God. Christians, of course, are bound to proclaim the unique role of Christ. They need not, however, also adopt John's exclusive dualism. While maintaining the essential role of Christ, they can nevertheless follow the guidance of the United States Bishops' Committee on the Liturgy when it directs preachers to respect the continuing validity of God's covenant with the Jewish people and their responsive faithfulness (*God's Mercy Endures Forever*, September 1988, #31g). Such contemporary teaching by the church directs preachers and catechists to interpret John's exclusive dualism in such a way that it does not lead Christians to conclude that Jews are rejected by God.

The first verses of this passage provide a basis on which such a positive interpretation can be built. Verses 14 and 15 draw a favorable parallel between Moses and Jesus. Just as the action of Moses in lifting up the bronze serpent brought healing to Israel in the wilderness, so the action of Jesus' being lifted up will bring salvation to all who believe. The Greek word for "lifted up" can refer both to someone being crucified and a ruler being enthroned. John intends both senses, using them to illustrate the saving action of Christ. The positive comparison between Moses' and Jesus' actions fosters a positive connection between Judaism and Christianity. Even though we as Christians hold the saving action of Jesus as the greatest expression of God's love, we continue to recognize the true presence of that love in the history of Israel, both in the time of Moses and in the Jewish faith today.

Rabbinic Notes on the Bronze Serpent: John 3:14–21

3:14–15: "And just as Moses lifted up the serpent in the wilderness, so must the Son of Man be lifted up, that whoever believes in him may have eternal life."

In Numbers 21:3–9, the story of Moses' raising of a bronze serpent on a pole in the desert is related. When the Israelites wandered in the desert, many were bitten by snakes as divine punishment for complaining faithlessly against God and Moses (Num 21:5–6), while angry at the quality of food and water, and alarmed by the prospect of dying in the wilderness. The kind of snake named was the "seraph," so called due to its legendary appearance with wings. As they were afflicted with the terrible bites, the Israelites then begged Moses for relief and God's forgiveness; Moses in turn besought God for help. The solution was to create an image of a bronze serpent, mounted on a pole; all who looked upon it would be cured (Num 21:9). Such an image, known by its Hebrew name of *nehas nehoshet,* or "bronze serpent," may have paralleled other guilt offerings made to God in expiation for offenses against the ark of the covenant (cf. 1 Sam 5:6 and 6:5). In all cases, the sinner was bidden to look upon the humanly made image, thereby acknowledging the power of the one, true God who saves and forgives. By looking in repentance upon the image of the poisonous serpent, viewers were also reversing the bitterness and rejection of God in their hearts that had occasioned their original punishment. By this, repentant Israelites were opening themselves to a right relationship with God, that is, to a cure of their affliction.

In the Mishnah, *Rosh ha-Shanah* 3.8, there is a brief discussion of this very serpent incident:

3.8: A. Now it happened that when Moses held up his hand, Israel prevailed, and when he let his hand fall, Amalek prevailed (Exodus 17.11).

B. Now do Moses' hands make war or stop it?

C. But the purpose is to say this to you:

D. So long as the Israelites would set their eyes upward and submit their hearts to their Father in heaven, they would grow stronger. And if not, they fell.

E. In like wise, you may say the following:

F. Make yourself a fiery serpent and set it on a standard, and it shall come to pass that every one who is bitten, when he sees it, shall live (Numbers 21.8).

G. Now does that serpent [on the standard] kill or give life? [Obviously not].

H. But: So long as the Israelites would set their eyes upward and submit to their Father in heaven, they would be healed. And if not, they would pine away.

(From Jacob Neusner's *The Mishnah: A New Translation* [New Haven: Yale University Press, 1988], 304–5)

This incident is referred to in Deuteronomy 8:15 as a reminder of the need for fidelity to the Law and gratitude to God for the Exodus. For some seven hundred years that followed, the same bronze image stood atop a pole before the Jerusalem Temple, only to be broken to pieces by King Hezekiah (2 Kgs 18:4), since by misuse it had been transformed into an idol—the exact opposite of its purpose in originally reminding its viewers to restore their faith and confidence in the one God of Israel.

In John 3:14–21, Jesus' self-comparison with the bronze serpent is unparalleled in Jewish literature. No references can be found to anyone making of himself a comparable symbol, especially through the dreaded Roman form of capital punishment, crucifixion. Jesus' astonishing teaching is that just as looking upon the bronze serpent with faith and repentance could bring healing to Israelites in the desert, so too, looking upon him fastened to the cross would bring eternal life (John 3:15).

16
Palm Sunday of the Lord's Passion, Cycle B • John 12:12–16

12:12When the great crowd that had come to the feast heard
  that Jesus was coming to Jerusalem,
    13they took palm branches and went out to meet him, and cried out:
    "Hosanna!
    "Blessed is he who comes in the name of the Lord,
      the king of Israel."

14Jesus found an ass and sat upon it, as is written:
    15*Fear no more, O daughter Zion;*
      see, your king comes, seated upon an ass's colt.
16His disciples did not understand this at first,
  but when Jesus had been glorified
  they remembered that these things were written about him
  and that they had done this for him.

In Cycle B, John's account of the triumphal entry into Jerusalem
is an option to be read before the procession with palms. An account
of the entry into Jerusalem is found in all four gospels. John, however,
has shaped his account to achieve a particular effect. In 12:13 John
adds the title, "king of Israel," to his quotation from Psalm 118:26. By
this addition the evangelist is emphasizing that the crowds are wel-
coming Jesus in a gesture of religious and nationalistic fervor.
Without a doubt John believes that Jesus is more than a nationalistic
king. He emphasizes the incompleteness of the crowd's belief when
he mentions that even the disciples did not understand the significance of the event until after Jesus was glorified (12:16).

Yet even if the crowd's acclamation falls short of the Johannine
standard, it remains a positive and believing response. In fact this scene
stands as one of the most vivid portrayals in the Gospel of a large group
of Jews acclaiming Jesus. Coming as it does before the accounts of the

passion during Holy Week, it provides an important corrective to the impression that "all the Jews" of Jesus' time rejected him. Although it is a frequent cliché in preaching and catechesis to suggest that the same crowd who hailed Jesus as their king would soon call for his death, this comment should be avoided. The crowd scenes that populate the Synoptic accounts of the passion are largely absent from John's account of Jesus' death. It is *hoi Ioudaioi* (often translated, "the Jews") who call for his execution. Once we understand, however, that *hoi Ioudaioi* refers to the Temple authorities, such scenes as the trial before Pilate are actually played out without the presence of a Jewish crowd.

Moreover, it would be historically impossible to establish that "the crowd" that appears in verse 12 was identical to the crowd that called for his death, especially if there is doubt that a Jewish crowd was ever present at Jesus' trial. It is better on historical and pastoral grounds to present the triumphal entry as a positive response by many of the Jews of Jesus' time and leave the responsibility for Jesus' death in the hands of Pilate and the Temple leadership cooperating with the Roman agenda.

Rabbinic Notes on the Entrance into Jerusalem: John 12:12–16

12:12–13: The next day the great crowd that had come to the festival heard that Jesus was coming to Jerusalem. So they took branches of palm trees and went out to meet him....

John's account of Jesus' entrance into Jerusalem is structured around two important scriptural quotations to portray him as the Messiah, or the promised one of Israel. As the crowd begins to shout out the text of Psalm 118:26—taken from the longest psalm in the Psalter and that most thankful to God for his Torah—palm branches are waved in salute to Jesus. Why was this? The books of the Maccabees (1 Macc 13:51 and 2 Macc 10:7) may provide some hint, in describing the use of palm branches this way in salute to a victory of Simon over those who held Jerusalem in 141 BCE. Again, when the Jews defeated Antiochus Epiphanes in approximately 162 BCE, Maccabeus himself purified the Temple, while the Jews waved palm branches—in imitation of the feast of Booths (to recall their deliverance from the desert where they had taken protection under huts built of branches)—and sang to God their hymns of praise for the exaltation of the holy city. In any case, the use of branches like these signals an important moment: that someone seen as a kind of leader or even liberator against unjust powers was entering into the city of Jerusalem. It is from this point of view that the Roman occupation must have looked askance at the arrival of Jesus in a week already charged with nationalistic feeling for the celebration of Passover. Josephus notes (*Wars* 5.243–4), for example, that because the law required Jewish men to come to Jerusalem annually for the Passover, there were many occasions when such feasts became opportunities for political protests against then-occupying forces. For Jews to wave palms at the arrival of Jesus certainly connoted a religio-political atmosphere to the occasion—one that would ultimately help to explain the severe Roman displeasure with the figure of Jesus as a potential enemy of Caesar, real or imagined. As the latest in a long history of anti-Jewish occupation forces, the Romans would have been alert to the frustration John puts into the mouths of those Pharisees who would ultimately cabal with the Romans at Jesus' trial: "Look, the world has gone after him!" (John 12:19).

12:13: [The crowd shouted,] "Hosanna! Blessed is the one who comes in the name of the Lord—the king of Israel!"
Here, John has conflated two scriptural texts to create a unique kind of acclamation for Jesus on the lips of Jews who welcomed him. First, he quotes, as mentioned above, from Psalm 118:25–26, heralding Jesus' arrival with the Hebrew word, "Hosanna!" which means "Lord, give salvation!" and was used in supplication before the king (2 Sam 14:4). The greeting of pilgrims who arrived in Jerusalem was not infrequently observed with the exclamation, "Blessed is he who comes in the name of the Lord" (cf. 2 Sam 6:18). John's addition of the phrase, "[even] the king of Israel"— possibly from Zephaniah 3:14–15—makes for a unique composition altogether and may need to be interpreted against his own admission in verse 16 that it was not until after Jesus' death that his disciples began to read the scriptures through the experiences of their master, allowing them to understand his actions as fulfilling the expectations of their ancestors.

12:14: Jesus found a young donkey and sat upon it: as is written....
The use of a donkey, as opposed to a great horse, was a sign of a peaceful and humble entrance. This contrasts starkly with the Roman triumphal practice of entering conquered cities—Jerusalem included—on horseback, glistening arms on display. In the Talmud, *Berakoth* 56b, the donkey is an animal whose appearance in a dream promises the hope of salvation. Jesus' depiction on "a don-

key's colt" is surely meant to evoke the messianic images associated with John's only partial use of the full quotation from Zechariah 9:9:

> Rejoice greatly, O daughter Zion!
>   Shout aloud, O daughter Jerusalem!
> Lo, your king comes to you;
>   triumphant and victorious is he,
> humble and riding on a donkey,
>   on a colt, the foal of a donkey.

Matthew's Gospel makes a similar use of this text at Matthew 21:2ff. (cf. Mark 11:2 and Luke 29:30). The point of the imagery is to depict a new kind of kingship for Jerusalem: one of peace and humility in service of the people.

17

The Eighteenth Sunday of the Year, Cycle B • John 6:24–35

^{6:24}When the crowd saw that neither Jesus nor his disciples were there,
they themselves got into boats
and came to Capernaum looking for Jesus.
²⁵And when they found him across the sea they said to him,
"Rabbi, when did you get here?"
²⁶Jesus answered them and said,
"Amen, amen, I say to you,
you are looking for me not because you saw signs
but because you ate the loaves and were filled.
²⁷Do not work for food that perishes
but for the food that endures for eternal life,
which the Son of Man will give you.
For on him the Father, God, has set his seal."
²⁸So they said to him,
"What can we do to accomplish the works of God?"
²⁹Jesus answered and said to them,
"This is the work of God, that you believe in the one he sent."
³⁰So they said to him,
"What sign can you do, that we may see and believe in you?
What can you do?
³¹Our ancestors ate manna in the desert, as it is written:
He gave them bread from heaven to eat."
³²So Jesus said to them,
"Amen, amen, I say to you,
it was not Moses who gave the bread from heaven;
my Father gives you the true bread from heaven.
³³For the bread of God is that which comes down from heaven
and gives life to the world."

³⁴So they said to him,
"Sir, give us this bread always."
³⁵Jesus said to them,

"I am the bread of life;
whoever comes to me will never hunger,
and whoever believes in me will never thirst."

The sixth chapter of John's Gospel centers around the theme of Jesus as the Bread of Life. One can also trace within it a growing opposition toward Jesus as the clarity of his identity increases. The lectionary has chosen segments of this chapter to be read in Cycle B from the seventeenth to the twenty-first Sundays of the year. Last Sunday, John's version of the multiplication of the loaves was read. This Sunday, Jesus begins a dialogue with the crowd that has followed him from that miraculous event. In verses 30–31 the crowd asks for a sign and cites the Hebrew scriptures to prove that their ancestors received bread from heaven. The citation that the crowd gives, "He gave them bread from heaven to eat," is not an exact rendering of any scriptural passage. John, however, has Jesus take up the citation and offer his own understanding of it in the manner of a typical Jewish interpreter. For John this scripture does not refer to a past gift of Moses but to a present gift of God. Remember that in these verses the "bread" that is being discussed most likely refers to God's revelation. Thus John is claiming that the true revelation was not the past Law (bread) of Moses but the present teaching (bread) of Jesus.

Preachers and catechists should approach the explanation of this text carefully. In the midst of an active debate with his opponents, the evangelist is clearly asserting the superiority of his community's understanding of Jesus over the revelation of the Torah. However, as a present-day minister holds up the unique importance of Christ for believers, he or she must not give the impression that the revelation of Moses is without value. As the 1985 Vatican "Notes on the Correct Way to Present the Jews and Judaism in Preaching and Catechesis in the Roman Catholic Church" reminds us, the Hebrew scriptures retain their own value as revelation (#7). With this awareness, those who interpret this Sunday's gospel should avoid presenting the revelation of Jesus as a replacement for Jewish faith. Rather, the revelation of Moses should be recognized as the foundation out of which Christianity emerged and a faith tradition that continues in its own right today.

NOTES ON DIETARY LAWS

Jesus' claim to be the Bread of Life provides an opportunity to discuss the Jewish laws concerning food.

Dietary laws are a collection of Jewish religious laws and customs relating to the types of food permitted for consumption. The Hebrew word for dietary laws is *kashrut,* derived from the root *kshar,* (fit or proper). The word appears in the Bible only three times: Esther 8:5; Ecclesiastes 10:10 and 11:6. The term, however, doesn't relate to food in these three biblical contexts. Elsewhere, however, the biblical text does describe permitted and nonpermitted dietary laws on meat, fruit, and vegetables. All vegetables and fish are permitted. Deuteronomy 14:6 stresses that animals that chew their cud and whose hooves are wholly cloven are clean for consumption. Animals that have only one of the required characteristics of biblical law, for example, the camel, which does not have split hooves, are forbidden to be eaten (Deut 14:7–8). The Bible enumerates forty-two "unclean" animals that cannot be eaten. Leviticus 11:13–19 lists twenty "unclean" birds and Deuteronomy 14:12–18 enumerates twenty-one. Based on the biblical account, the rabbis and scholars compiled a total of twenty-four "unclean" birds (Tractate *Hullin*— Animals Killed for Food—63a/b). Concerning fish, only those that have only one fin and one easily removable scale can be cleaned and permitted, as pointed out by Leviticus 11:9–12. Some insects are permitted to be eaten, especially four kinds of locusts, as pointed out in Leviticus 11:21–22. The preparation of meat follows a strict procedure. It is essentially a prohibition against the consumption of blood as pointed out in Leviticus 7:26–27; 17:11–14. The purpose of the process of koshering is to draw out and drain the meat of all the blood that can be removed. It is done by salting the meat or by roasting it over an open flame. It is forbidden to eat meat and milk together. The texts of Exodus 23:19; 34:26 and Deuteronomy 14:21 strongly say, "You shall not boil a kid in its mother's milk." There is a theory that the reason for this biblical prohibition was to avoid any comparison with a similar sacrifice in local non-Jewish customs of mixing the kid in its mother's milk. In that way, the biblical and rabbinic scholars eliminated any possibility of imagining, by eating in such a way, that anyone might offer a sacrifice to the local gods. The prophets referred to the laws of *kashrut* in many texts. For example, Ezekiel 4:14 says, "Then I said, 'Ah, Lord God! I have never defiled myself; from my youth up until now I have never eaten what died of itself or was torn by animals, nor has carrion flesh come into my mouth.'" Daniel and his friends refused to partake of the "royal rations of food and wine" (Dan 1:8). In the days of Jesus, *kashrut* was central in daily Jewish spirituality. Jesus, himself, followed the laws as part of his spiritual commitment and a way of religious discipline. There was among some the feeling that following *kashrut* would separate a person from the society at large. The Book of Tobit 1:10–11 stresses the difference as a way to project the covenantal relationship with God. It says, "[E]veryone of my kindred and my people ate the food of the Gentiles, but I kept myself from eating the food of the Gentiles."

Both biblical and rabbinic sources attempt to explain the dietary laws. Exodus 22:31 says, "You shall be a people consecrated to me; therefore, you shall not eat any meat that is mangled by beasts in the field; you shall throw it to the dogs." Leviticus 11:44–45 stresses, "For I am the LORD your God; sanctify yourselves therefore, and be holy, for I am holy. You shall not defile yourselves with any swarming creature that moves on the earth." Deuteronomy 14:21 says, "You shall not eat anything that dies of itself; you may give it to aliens residing in your towns for them to eat, or you may sell it to a foreigner. For you are a people holy to the LORD your God." The rabbinic sources, mainly Talmud, *Yoma*—The Day of Atonement—76b, stress that the dietary laws are "divine statutes," which, by definition, are not explained in the text. They are moral consequences in the keeping of *kashrut*. In Ezekiel 33:25, the prophet equates the eating of blood with a sense of idolatry and murder. Aristeas, an Egyptian Jew who probably lived in the first century BCE, said that the dietary laws are meant to inspire men with a spirit of justice and to teach them certain moral lessons (the Letter of Aristeas 42–7). The rabbis of the Talmud did not try to explain the dietary laws. They said that "for that what does the Holy One, blessed be He, care whether a man kills an animal by the throat or by the nape of its neck. Hence, its purpose is to refine man" (Genesis Rabbah 44:1; Leviticus Rabbah 13:3). The mystics thought that the keeping of the laws of *kashrut* has positive effects on the character and spirituality of a person. Rabbi Samson Raphael Hirsch, in his book, *Horeb* (section 454), explains *kashrut:* "Just as the human spirit is the instrument which God uses to make himself known in this world, so the human body is the medium which connects the outside world with the mind of man.... [A]nything which gives the body too much independence or makes it too active in carnal direction, brings it near to the animal's fear, thereby robbing it of its primary function, to be the intermediary between the soul of man and the world outside. Bearing in mind this function of the body and also the fact that the physical structure of man is largely influenced by the kind of food he consumes, one might come to the conclusion that the vegetable food is the most preferable as plants are the most passive substance; and indeed, in Jewish law, all vegetables are permitted without discrimination." There is also a hygienic explanation that is stated in Maimonides' *Guide of the Perplexed,* 3:48. The Spanish-Jewish philosopher and law scholar said: "These ordinances seek to train us in the mastery of our appetites. They accustom us to restrain both the growth of desire and the disposition to consider the pleasure of eating as the end of man's existence." Maimonides also stressed: "All the food which the Torah has forbidden us to eat has some bad and damaging effect on the body.... [T]he principal reason why the Law forbids swine's flesh is to be found in the circumstances that its habits and its food are very dirty and loathsome." He adds that "the fat of the intestines is forbidden because it fattens and destroys the abdomen and creates cold and clammy blood." He finally states, referring to the question of meat and milk, that "meat boiled in milk is undoubtedly gross food and makes a person feel overfull." However, he explains, "I think that most probably it is also prohibited because it is somehow connected with idolatry. Perhaps it was part of the ritual of certain pagan festivals. I find support for this view in the fact that two of the times the Lord mentions the prohibition that it is after the commandment concerning our festivals." "Three times a year all your males shall appear before the Lord, your God" (Exodus 17:23-24; 23:17), which is to say, "When you come before me on your festivals, do not prepare your food in the manner in which the heathens do" (Ibid. 3:48). The ancient inscriptions, for example, in Ras Shamra-Ugarit, tend to confirm that the custom of eating milk and meat together was related to a fertility rite.

18
The Nineteenth Sunday of the Year, Cycle B • John 6:41–51

⁶:⁴¹The Jews murmured about Jesus because he said,
  "I am the bread that came down from heaven,"
⁴²and they said,
  "Is this not Jesus, the son of Joseph?
Do we not know his father and mother?
Then how can he say,
  'I have come down from heaven'?"
⁴³Jesus answered and said to them,
  "Stop murmuring among yourselves.
⁴⁴No one can come to me unless the Father who sent me draw him,
  and I will raise him on the last day.
⁴⁵It is written in the prophets:
  They shall all be taught by God.
Everyone who listens to my Father and learns from him comes to me.
⁴⁶Not that anyone has seen the Father
  except the one who is from God;
  he has seen the Father.
⁴⁷Amen, amen, I say to you,
  whoever believes has eternal life.
⁴⁸I am the bread of life.
⁴⁹Your ancestors ate the manna in the desert, but they died;
  ⁵⁰this is the bread that comes down from heaven
  so that one may eat it and not die.
⁵¹I am the living bread that came down from heaven;
  whoever eats this bread will live forever;
  and the bread that I will give is my flesh for the life
    of the world."

In this section of the Bread of Life discourse, the opposition to Jesus' identity and teaching increases. Moreover, the identity of Jesus' opponents changes. No longer are they "the crowd," as they were in last week's lectionary selection. Now it is *hoi Ioudaioi* who complain. As we explained in the Introduction, although *hoi Ioudaioi* is usually translated as "the Jews," its polemical sense regularly carries a much more limited referent. Most frequently that referent is the Temple authorities in Jerusalem. However, the occurrence of *hoi Ioudaioi* in verse 41 of today's Gospel together with another occurrence in next week's lectionary selection (6:52) are two instances in which the referent seems to be the crowd with whom Jesus is debating. These two polemical occurrences of *hoi Ioudaioi* are the only ones that occur outside of Judea. (The setting here is Galilee.) This has led some commentators to suggest that the term's presence in this chapter reflects the hand of a later editor of the Gospel. However we explain the presence of *hoi Ioudaioi* in these verses, we can recognize the same tendency found in other sections of John's Gospel: *Hoi Ioudaioi* suddenly replaces another group. Therefore, a more precise rendering of *hoi Ioudaioi* in 6:41 and 6:52 would be "some in the crowd."

As in most cases when *hoi Ioudaioi* occurs within a reading, the preacher or catechist should attempt to blunt the general impression given by most translations that Jesus was opposed by the Jewish people as a whole. This can be done by making the conscious decision in our preaching and teaching to refer to Jesus' questioners and opponents in terms other than "the Jews."

19
The Twentieth Sunday of the Year, Cycle B • John 6:51–58

Today's selection from John is a continuation of Jesus' Bread of Life discourse from the previous Sundays. Verse 6:52 contains one polemical use of *hoi Ioudaioi* that seems to refer to some of those in the crowd. See the discussion in the commentary for the Nineteenth Sunday of the Year in Cycle B, above.

20
Christ the King, Cycle B
John 18:33–37

The gospel reading for this feast is taken from the passion of John. The preacher or catechist should be aware of the anti-Jewish potential in verse 35, "Your own nation and the chief priests handed you over to me," and verse 36 where *hoi Ioudaioi* is used to identify those to whom Jesus has been handed over. For a discussion of these verses, please consult the commentary for Good Friday.

21
Solemnity of the Most Sacred Heart of Jesus, Cycle B • John 19:31–37

The lectionary selection for this feast is taken from the passion narrative of John. It includes a use of *hoi Ioudaioi*. "The Jews" are said to ask Pilate that the legs of those crucified be broken so that the bodies would not remain on the cross on the Sabbath. As discussed in "Negative Factors toward Jews and Judaism in John's Presentation of Jesus' Passion and Death" (see Good Friday, above), *hoi Ioudaioi* refers here not to "all Jews" but to the Temple authorities.

22
November 2, All Souls, Cycles A, B, C

If option 9 (John 6:51–59) is chosen for the gospel, it contains a polemical use of *hoi Ioudaioi*. Refer to the treatment of this passage at the Nineteenth and Twentieth Sundays of the Year, Cycle B, above.

If option 10 (John 11:17–27) or option 11 (John 11:32–45) is chosen, refer to the treatment for the Fifth Sunday of Lent, Cycle A. There, positive possibilities for the use of *hoi Ioudaioi* are discussed.

23
November 9, The Dedication of the Lateran Basilica, Cycles A, B, C
John 2:13–22

This selection is the same as that used on the Third Sunday of Lent, Cycle B.

Readings from the Gospel of John in Cycle C

24
The Second Sunday of the Year, Cycle C • John 2:1–11

$^{2:1}$There was a wedding at Cana in Galilee,
   and the mother of Jesus was there.
^{2}Jesus and his disciples were also invited to the wedding.
^{3}When the wine ran short,
   the mother of Jesus said to him,
   "They have no wine."
^{4}And Jesus said to her,
   "Woman, how does your concern affect me?
My hour has not yet come."
^{5}His mother said to the servers,
   "Do whatever he tells you."
^{6}Now there were six stone water jars there for Jewish ceremonial washings,
   each holding twenty to thirty gallons.
^{7}Jesus told them,
   "Fill the jars with water."
So they filled them to the brim.
^{8}Then he told them,
   "Draw some out now and take it to the headwaiter."
So they took it.
^{9}And when the headwaiter tasted the water that had become wine,
   without knowing where it came from
   —although the servers who had drawn the water knew—,
   the headwaiter called the bridegroom ^{10}and said to him,
   "Everyone serves good wine first,
   and then when people have drunk freely, an inferior one;
   but you have kept the good wine until now."
^{11}Jesus did this as the beginning of his signs at Cana in Galilee
   and so revealed his glory,
   and his disciples began to believe in him.

The account of the marriage feast at Cana is clearly stated by John as the first of Jesus' signs (2:11). In the midst of this sign, use is made of six stone jars that were used for the Jewish rites of purification (2:6). The symbolism of turning the water in these jars into the finest of wines introduces a theme that can be found throughout the Gospel: Jesus replaces Jewish practices and institutions.

Since this theme is only stated symbolically in this passage, the danger of anti-Jewish bias is minimal. Nevertheless, as the preacher or catechist draws out the meaning of the story, care must be taken not to imply a rejection of Judaism or a termination of its religious practices. The 2001 statement of the Pontifical Biblical Commission ("The Jewish People and Their Scriptures in the Christian Bible," #36) reminds the pastoral minister that the New Testament never says that Israel has been rejected by God. Therefore, even as we joyously partake of the new wine that Jesus offers us, we should in no way undermine the truth that the Jewish faith and its religious traditions continue as a source of spiritual life.

MOSAIC LAW

In the past, many inadequate readings of the Hebrew Bible have maintained that the Law of Moses was preoccupied with a vicious legalism. This unfortunate idea became an important element in a tradition of contempt for the biblical text and Judaism itself. The study of the Bible, especially the Jewish commentaries expounding the meaning of the word of God, showed the interest of performing God's commandments and religious, legal statutes with love, trying to implement the presence of God in daily and community life. This process started with God himself, who in Jeremiah 31:31–33 proclaims the renewal of the covenant through the commitment of the Jewish community. The text says, "The days are surely coming, says the LORD, when I will make a new covenant with the house of Israel and the house of Judah. It will not be like the covenant that I made with their ancestors when I took them by the hand to bring them out of the land of Egypt—a covenant that they broke, though I was their husband, says the LORD. But this is the covenant that I will make with the house of Israel after those days, says the LORD: I will put my law within them, and I will write it on their hearts." This is the beginning of a whole process of commentary and making the word of God meaningful for each generation. It was expressed by Ezra and Nehemiah after the Babylonian Exile. Both returned to Jerusalem and rebuilt it, as well as the Temple. They reorganized the political structure of the new community according to Torah precepts, that is, according to the first five books of the Jewish Bible. Ezra and Nehemiah represented the two main aspects of the people's lives: Ezra represented the spiritual renewal, and Nehemiah the political reorganization. Ezra discussed religious duties, liturgical and ritual, but also started the process of expounding the meaning of a scripture, especially the Book of Deuteronomy. His explorations were attempts to interpret the text in order to enact the sacredness of the God-Israel relationship, bringing about a sense of holiness in daily life, both for the Jewish person and for the community. Ezra started the process of interpretation as pointed out in Nehemiah 7:73—8:3: "When the seventh month came—the people of Israel being settled in their towns—all the people gathered together into the square before the Water Gate. They told the scribe Ezra to bring the book of the law of Moses, which the LORD had given to Israel. Accordingly, the priest Ezra brought the law before the assembly, both men and women and all who could hear with understanding. This was on the first day of the seventh month. He read from it facing the square before the Water Gate from early morning until midday." Ezra started the process of explanation and interpretation that would engage teachers and scribes for several centuries up to the days of Jesus and afterward. The tradition of Oral Law transmitted by generations of interpreters resulted in two bodies of rabbinic religious thought. One covered religious legislation, the Mishnah, dealing with all aspects of life: the life of prayer and religious festivals, birth and death, marriage and divorce, business matters, and so on. The other was the Midrash, the literary existential explanation of biblical stories, a commentary read and discussed in the synagogue and deeply imbued with an ethical message. The Midrash influenced Jesus' message and the gospel writing. Interpretation inevitably involves a reshaping of the text to make it meaningful for the present. Professor Simon Rawidowicz defines it as a "revolution from within," an enterprise that reshapes the spirituality and actuality of God's word and covenant. Professor Rawidowicz states:

> Interpretation lives by crisis in various degrees. The crisis that stimulates it will become its criterion. Interpretation can be characterized by a particular attitude of the interpreter who struggles between preserving and rejecting some forms of content of the word at his interpretive "mercy," by attention between continuation and rebellion, tradition and innovation.

It derives its strength from both a deep attachment to the "text" and from an "alienation" from it, a certain distance, a gap which has to be breached. Interpretation is the "way out" when man is compelled to "take it" or "break it." Many a battle was fought and lost on the battlefield of interpretation. And the battle goes on and will go on as long as this person is an interpreter.

Jesus followed this tradition and interpreted and reinterpreted the text of the Hebrew Bible according to his own reading, vocation, and religious commitment.

Rabbinic Notes on the Wedding Feast at Cana: John 2:1–11

There are several important features of Judaism presented by John in this story. First, the customs involved at a Jewish wedding form the immediate backdrop for the actions of Jesus. Most important is the fact that Jesus and his mother, as well as his disciples, have all been invited to a particular wedding at which the wine supply has run out. It is important to note the words of the wine steward—"But you have kept the good wine until now" (2:10)—clearly suggesting that the feast was well along in its normal course when the wine supply ran low. Wedding feasts often ran for seven days, judging by the testimony in Judges 14:12 and Tobit 11:19, especially for the wedding of a virgin (Mishnah, *Ketuboth* 1). This would mean that Jesus is prevailed upon somewhere near the end of "the bridal week" (cf. Gen 29:27)—a time at which the guests are looking toward the formal close of the celebration and their own return home. Surely this would be the moment for the lesser wines?

But it is also quite possible that John has purposely charged the entire scene with messianic imagery in connection with his own belief that Jesus is himself the Messiah, the long-awaited one, whose appearance will mark an age of expectations fulfilled, often portrayed in terms of a wedding banquet. In Isaiah 54:4–8, for example, and again at 62:4–5, we see the theme of a wedding banquet as the setting for the reconciliation of Israel with God, who welcomes her back from infidelity and sinfulness. At Qumran, the same central idea is present, that the Messiah will dine with his followers both so as to participate in as well as anticipate the full reign of God on the earth (1Qumran Scroll a 2.11–22). At his final Passover meal, Jesus makes a kind of messianic allusion to the food that shall be eaten and drunk finally within the kingdom that is to come

(Luke 22:16–18). And again at Matthew 9:14–16, Jesus clearly puts forward the wedding feast as the primary analogue for the coming of the Messiah and the fulfillment of God's promises.

But, as Roger Aus has pointed out in his intriguing study of this story (*Water into Wine and the Beheading of John the Baptist* [Atlanta: Scholars Press, 1988]) there is yet another story in the Bible in which the drinking of "old" rather than "new" wine at a wedding feast can help to explain the Cana story that features Jesus so prominently in the same themes. It is that of Esther, as she dines at the wedding of King Ahasuerus, as found in Esther 1:1–8. There, Esther is a guest at the marriage of Ahasuerus and his wife, Vashti, both Persians. In the Jewish *Haggadah* or Midrash on this passage (Esther Rabbah 2–4), the surprise for all the guests is that the last day of the feast is like the first: excellent in all its food and drink, contrary to custom, and perhaps even to common sense. For the rabbis who read and taught about Esther, the idea that the last day was as good as the first was indeed a sign of the messianic banquet, whose abundance would know no end. It is likely this was the background that John had in mind when he put an expression in the mouth of the wine steward at the wedding of Cana so much like that of the banqueter of Ahasuerus: "Everyone serves the good wine first, and then the inferior wine after the guests have become drunk. But you have kept the good wine until now" (John 2:10).

A second important Jewish feature of the story that Aus has highlighted is found in the exchanges between Jesus and Mary, and then between Mary and the servants. Given in the most formal of terms, she is described here not by name, but by the honored title of "the mother of Jesus" (v. 3). Continuing the formality, Jesus addresses her as "Woman" (v. 4)—again, evidencing deep regard—but adds a question in a very Jewish turn of phrase or "Semiticism": "What concern is that to you and to me?" (v. 4) This same expression can also be found in Judges 11:12, 2 Chronicles 30:21, and 1 Kings 17:18. In these places, this turn of phrase functions like a mild puzzlement: What is it that you really want of me? In other references, such as 2 Kings 3:13 or Hosea 14:8, it takes on a slightly more neutral tone: Is this matter really my business? The ambiguity of the expression is used by Jesus to suggest that the problem at hand is not simply his own to solve. By this easily identifiable expression, John portrayed Jesus as one whose mission is received from God, rather than being self-determined. Indeed, Jesus' response reflects a kind of holy indifference to Mary's remark, unless it corresponded—as John's story attempts to

bear out—to the arrival of the "messianic" signs that Jesus' followers longed to see.

Mary's final direction to the servants—"Do whatever he tells you"
(v. 5)—is, again, reminiscent of the Esther story mentioned above.
There, at Esther 1:8, Ahasuerus orders the stewards to "do as each
one desired"—that is, to supply them with as much to drink as they
could possibly desire. Could it be that, in continuing the midrashic
theme he has introduced, John places the words of the king in the
mouth of the mother of Jesus? It might seem so, for the entire story
of Cana appears to come together best if it can be understood in
light of a messianic-style banquet already familiar to Jewish readers
of John.

A third element of Judaism can be found in the fact that Jewish
rites of purification are suddenly in the fore when John mentions in
verse six that there were, in fact, six stone water jars at hand, each
of which could hold twenty or thirty gallons—a very large amount
indeed. What were such jars doing there? The laws regulating
impurity in Leviticus 11 through 15 are probably invoked by this
passage, with the prescription that a clay jar that has been used
for holding water must be broken if it were to be contaminated
under the prescriptions of the Law (Lev 11:29–33). Stone jars,
however, do not carry this burden, for they could not be made
"unclean" in the same sense and were, as a result, much preferred.
The Mishnah, *Betzah* 2.3 details this belief. The most ordinary
purification of Jewish houseguests was probably indicated by the
presence of these jars: the washing of feet after a journey, as well as
the washing of hands before eating (cf. Mark 7:1–6). But why would
John portray the water for *purification* as the stuff of Jesus' own
"messianic" wine?

Again, Aus's thesis may assist us here by demonstrating that the
story of Esther at the wedding of Ahasuerus provides us with the key
to our mystery. Jesus' curious command to the servants in John's
story—"Now standing there were six stone water jars for the Jewish
rites of purification, each holding twenty or thirty gallons. Jesus
said to them, 'Fill the jars with water'" (v. 6–7)—would suggest
something that could be easily missed by the reader: Up to that
point in the story, at least, the jars were empty. They held nothing,
needing to be filled, if used at all. Jesus, then, is not transforming
what is already in use at a Jewish wedding. Rather, he purposely
chooses the framework of purification (from vessels yet to be pre-
pared at that!) as the context from which his abundant "messianic"
wine will be offered. This small feature intrigues because it sug-

gests that Jesus would begin his signs with a profound respect for that which is ritually pure, fit for consumption under the Law, and free of all defilement. By choosing as he did, Jesus demonstrated a very close connection in his own thinking between who and what he was as a Jew—including his observance of the Law and its meaning—with what he would envision as his own mission to the house of Israel.

25
The Fifth Sunday of Lent, Cycle C
John 8:1–11

8:1Jesus went to the Mount of Olives.
2But early in the morning he arrived again in the temple area,
    and all the people started coming to him,
    and he sat down and taught them.
3Then the scribes and the Pharisees brought a woman
    who had been caught in adultery
    and made her stand in the middle.
4They said to him,
    "Teacher, this woman was caught
    in the very act of committing adultery.
5Now in the law, Moses commanded us to stone such women.
So what do you say?"
6They said this to test him,
    so that they could have some charge to bring against him.
Jesus bent down and began to write on the ground with his finger.
7But when they continued asking him,
    he straightened up and said to them,
    "Let the one among you who is without sin
    be the first to throw a stone at her."
8Again he bent down and wrote on the ground.
9And in response, they went away one by one,
    beginning with the elders.
So he was left alone with the woman before him.
10Then Jesus straightened up and said to her,
    "Woman, where are they?
Has no one condemned you?"
11She replied, "No one, sir."
Then Jesus said, "Neither do I condemn you.
Go, and from now on do not sin any more."

      There is general scholarly agreement that this story is not a part of the original Gospel of John. It is missing from the earliest manu-

134

scripts of the Gospel. However, since our present canon has associated it with John, it will be treated here.

This story of Jesus and the woman who was charged with adultery is both beautiful and poignant. It highlights Jesus' forgiveness and compassion for sinners. In this regard it is similar to many well-loved passages from Luke, such as the stories of Zacchaeus (Luke 19:1–10) and the repentant thief (Luke 23:39–43). Unlike those stories, however, this passage is preserved in the form of a controversy dialogue. This type of narrative form portrays Jesus in argumentation with his opponents. Since the New Testament is Christian literature, Jesus invariably wins. For the same reason, the opponents of Jesus are usually colored negatively, though they often initially hold the upper hand.

This is the case in our present passage. Jesus' opponents attempt to entrap him (8:6). Moreover, if we presume a context in which the Temple leadership did not have the authority to pass the death sentence without the Roman governor's approval (John 19:31b), Jesus' opponents present him with a dilemma. If he condemns the woman, he violates Roman law. If he pardons her, he contradicts Mosaic Law. To the delight of the reader who is supportive of Jesus, he defeats his opponents without falling into the trap. Similar to the controversy dialogue concerning the payment of taxes to the emperor (Mark 12:13–17), Jesus wins without passing a direct judgment. He defeats his opponents with superior insight and authority.

Aware of the literary form of the controversy dialogue, the preacher or catechist should be wary of extending the evil motives of Jesus' opponents to all those who might have debated with him during his historical ministry. We have noted in the Introduction the tendency to shift the identity of Jesus' opponents within John's Gospel. Similar tendencies can be presumed in this passage. Therefore, even though verse 3 identifies Jesus' opponents as "the scribes and the Pharisees," one cannot conclude with certainty that scribes and Pharisees were Jesus' primary opponents during his ministry. One certainly cannot conclude that *all* the scribes and the Pharisees sought to engage Jesus with the underhanded motivation that this controversy dialogue sets forth.

In addition, those who preach and teach this passage should not use it to support the misconception that the Mosaic Law was legalistic or vicious. The deficiency in this story is not located in the law but rather in the opponents as colored by the controversy dialogue. The point of the story after all is not that adultery is of no import or that there should be no consequences for engaging in it. The point is that Jesus reflects the mercy of God to sinners, a God who will always find a way to rescue the lost, even in the face of clever opposition.

Rabbinic Notes on the Woman Caught in Adultery: John 8:1–11

8:2: Early in the morning he came again to the temple. All the people came to him and he sat down and began to teach them.

Jesus' presence in the Temple at the start of the story would help to suggest a legitimacy to his role as a teacher and judge. It is under these circumstances that the rabbi is then approached with a case on which to pass judgment: A woman has been taken in adultery and her apparent witnesses have brought her before Jesus with the question of whether she shouldn't be stoned to death in punishment, as prescribed by the Law of Moses. It should be carefully noted that Jesus seats himself, as would be expected of a teacher. His several changes of position later in the story (from sitting to standing, then stooping down to the ground, and finally to standing again) underline for his audience the different roles Jesus wishes to assume relative to the trial of this woman.

8:3: The scribes and the Pharisees brought a woman who had been caught in adultery; and [made] her stand before all of them.

John remarks that "scribes and Pharisees" are among those who have brought this woman to the rabbi. Scribes, as Temple officials, would have been involved in such a case routinely; their presence should not be seen as unusual, especially given Jesus' use of the Temple precincts. But what does it mean that "Pharisees" have presented this case to the rabbi? Readers must remember that there were seven different schools of Pharisees in Israel at the time of Jesus, and that his own teaching—in some ways so much like that of certain Pharisees—put him at variance with a number of them. By no means, however, were all Pharisees hostile to Jesus; Nicodemus, whom John describes in chapter three of his Gospel (John 3:1–21), was himself a Pharisee who was fascinated with the teachings of Jesus. Hence, the fact that some Pharisees have brought a case before Jesus should not be seen as a pretext for anti-Judaism even in the mind of the evangelist.

8:4: "Teacher, this woman was caught in the very act of committing adultery."

Here we are meant to understand that the woman was witnessed (as required in the law at Deuteronomy19:5) in a forbidden act. Normally, at least two witnesses were required to establish the probability of an adulterous act. According to the Mishnah, which may have reflected rabbinic thought at the time of Jesus, a concern for the fairness and accuracy of the accusation was seen in the demand for truthful witnesses. The text of *Sotah* 1.1–2 is explicit in this regard: "One who warned his wife—Rabbi Eliezer says: He must warn her in the presence of two witnesses, but he can give her to drink [the bitter waters] on the testimony of one witness of [even] his own testimony." By "bitter waters" is meant the mixture of water from a holy vessel used in the Temple for sanctification purposes, together with soil from the floor of the sanctuary. These two ingredients were then mixed in any earthenware vessel and became the drink offered to the alleged adulteress. They are called "bitter waters" since they have the potential—in the case of a truly guilty adulteress—allegedly to cause death or a bitter end. Before she drank the potion, the cohen or priest would read from the text of the Torah at Numbers 5:18, which cursed her as she drank, should she be guilty. In the story at hand, it may be presumed that those who have brought the woman to Jesus are themselves witnesses, ready to testify to her misdeeds. In addition, we are being told by this passage that she was neither raped nor coerced in any way, since Numbers 5:13 and Deuteronomy 22:23–27 would not punish her if she were somehow a victim rather than a consensual partner in an extramarital sexual act.

8:5: Now in the law, Moses commanded us to stone such women.

Under biblical law, a wife did not enjoy a reciprocal claim on the fidelity of her husband. As a result, a married man could take an unmarried woman as a mistress and not be in violation of the law, but a married woman could never take a lover and not expect to break the law in so doing. Understood within this context, then, adultery was forbidden by the Law of Moses in the Decalogue at Exodus 20:13 and Deuteronomy 5:17. In Leviticus 20:10 and Deuteronomy 22:21–22 both the man and the woman could be executed for this crime. Death by stoning was prescribed as the punishment for adulterers because it allowed for the participation of the entire community, since adultery was seen to be a crime that, like blasphemy, threatened communal life or identity. Jesus himself was similarly threatened by crowds in Jerusalem that had accused him of blasphemy, though he escaped from the stoning unhurt by hiding in the Temple area (John 8:59).

8:6a: They said this to test him, so that they might have some charge to bring against him.

Here we see a long-standing practice for challenging an enemy in the public square: framing a question in such a way that any answer given would indict. These types of questions, often built on what seemed insoluble legal, moral, or theological riddles, are found throughout the gospels (cf. Matt 12:10–14; 22:23–33; Mark 12:13–17). However, even Jesus uses the same technique with others (cf. Luke 14:1–6), though his opponents are often left without answers for the rabbi. In the present case, Jesus' challengers want him to choose between confirming the punishment of the law (and thereby refuting his own torah) or asserting the superiority of his own torah (and thereby subordinating Jewish law to human authority—all done within the Temple!) Jesus, however, refuses to participate, and effectively recasts the central question of the case *on terms intended to refocus the issue at hand*. In doing so, Jesus shows himself as much a master of this questioning technique as anyone, while at the same time escaping the conundrum posed for him. The entire process is meant to demonstrate how some Jewish practices worked in connection with legal controversy; in no way are these exchanges—sometimes marked by cleverness and harsh riposte—either anti-Jewish or anti-Christian thereby. Instead, the attempt to discomfit the rabbi—and his effort to confound his confounders—would have been seen as part and parcel of any trial.

8:6b: Jesus bent down and wrote with his finger on the ground.

What is the rabbi doing here? The best way to understand this is to return for a moment to the setting of the story: Jesus, as a rabbi or teacher, is holding forth in the Temple (the seat of true teaching), and is presented with a case in which to demonstrate his own teaching and its relationship to the Torah. While Jesus could be simply doodling in the sand, it is more likely that he was silently reminding everyone present of the text of Jeremiah 17:13 (emphasis added): "[T]hose who turn away from you shall be recorded in the underworld, for they have forsaken the *fountain of living water,* the LORD." Jesus engages in this gesture not once, but twice within this story, as if to underline his meaning as dramatically as possible. Quietly invoking this passage from Jeremiah would be in keeping with the ability of Jesus to recast the meaning of the entire scene on his own terms, and to subtly reintroduce into the minds of his onlookers a favorite theme in his own teaching: torah as living water. Indeed, Jesus' is the "torah of living water" throughout the Gospel of John, as seen repeatedly in stories such as that of the Samaritan woman at the well (John 4:1–42). Jesus has even equated himself and his torah with just such a fountain (John 4:14), available to all who wish it. We must return for a moment to reflect upon his change of position. As in accord with rabbinic custom, the judge would write his sentence down before standing to pronounce it.

8:7: Let anyone among you who is without sin be the first to throw a stone at her.

Here, Jesus is alluding to the method of stoning to be followed in such cases as described in Deuteronomy 13:10 and 17:17, where the witnesses to the crime must themselves be the first to cast stones at the adulterer. Jesus' challenging use of these verses from Deuteronomy implicitly asks: Who can be a witness against this woman when God is a witness against everyone? This is a beautiful teaching and represents not a rejection of the Torah, but a merciful way in which to see its application in the circumstances Jesus was asked to judge.

8:10–11: "Has no one condemned you?" She said, "No one, sir." And Jesus said, "Neither do I condemn you. Go your way, and from now on do not sin again."

This ending should be compared with Daniel 13:41, 48, and 53 and the trial of Susannah, unjustly accused of adultery. The word found in the Septuagint for condemnation is the same that Jesus uses here: In effect, he sets aside any right as a teacher to pass judgment on the accused woman. The entire story, then, begins and ends on the same theme of the rabbi as teacher and judge whose torah is put to the test in the practical order. Jesus' refusal to assume the role of judge as offered to him would appear to be intended as a further development of his own unique torah on the mercy of God toward sinners.

Study Questions

INTRODUCTION TO THE GOSPEL OF JOHN

1) What are the three stages in the development of the gospels as outlined by the Pontifical Biblical Commission (1964)? What are the implications of these stages?

2) In stage one of the gospel tradition, briefly describe how each of the following were understood: Judaism, Sadducees, Pharisees, Essenes, Zealots, Roman imperialism, Jesus, the opponents of Jesus.

3) What are some of the distinctive characteristics of the Gospel of John?

4) Why is dualism a central characteristic of the Gospel of John?

5) How does the history of the Johannine community reflect the composition of the Gospel of John?

6) How should texts referring to Jews in the New Testament be clarified in order to avoid confusion and contempt?

7) What role does opposition play in the Gospel of John?

8) How are the Jewish opposition groups—the chief priests *(archiereus)*, the authorities *(hoi archontes)*, and the Pharisees—portrayed?

9) Briefly describe the problematic issues associated with the translation, use of, and various understandings of the term *hoi Ioudaioi.*

10) Compare the neutral sense with the polemical sense of *hoi Ioudaioi.*

11) What are some of the pastoral sensitivities in the use of *hoi Ioudaioi*?

12) What is the retrograding tendency in the Gospel of John?

READINGS FROM THE GOSPEL OF JOHN IN CYCLE A

Chapters 1 and 2: John 1:1–18: Christmas and Second Sunday after Christmas

1) What are the two verses with potential for anti-Jewish bias in this section?
2) What are some ways for a preacher or catechist to show pastoral sensitivity in proclaiming the Christmas message?
3) How does John value the role of Moses?

Chapter 3: John 13:1–15: Holy Thursday, Mass of the Lord's Supper

1) How does this passage highlight the important notions of "clean" and "unclean" in Jewish life?
2) What is the significance of this "washing" and why does Jesus see it as essential?
3) How may a preacher or catechist make use of the reference to Passover?

Chapter 4: John 18:1 — 19:42: Good Friday

1) What are the historical circumstances of the death of Jesus?
2) How does one resolve the deicide accusation, given the past history?
3) How does the Gospel of John describe Jewish opposition to Jesus and involvement in his death? What role does Pontius Pilate play?
4) What are some ways for preachers and catechists to portray a more historically accurate understanding of Roman and Jewish involvement in the suffering and death of Jesus?
5) How is the Jewish practice of immediate burial after death conveyed in this section?
6) How does John the evangelist make use of symbolism in this Gospel passage?
7) What are some of the positive and negative factors in John's presentation of the passion and death of Jesus?
8) How is *hoi Ioudaioi* used in this section?

Chapter 5: John 20:19–31: Second Sunday of Easter

1) Why is the reference to the disciples behind locked doors "for fear of the Jews" inaccurate?

2) How does this section relate to the experience of a later historical Johannine community?

3) How may the greeting "Peace to you" be viewed?

4) What is the image of receiving the Holy Spirit conveyed in
other scripture references?

5) In what ways may "binding" and "loosening" be understood?

6) What is the connection between sight and belief?

Chapter 6: John 10: 1–10: Fourth Sunday of Easter

How does the inclusion of the term *Pharisees* into this lectionary
text reaffirm a common misunderstanding of the Pharisees?

Chapter 7: John 20:19-23: Pentecost Sunday

See questions in Cycle A: Second Sunday of Easter

Chapter 8: John 4:5–42: Third Sunday of Lent

1) What is the historical role and understanding in the relationship between Samaritans and Jews?

2) Why is it important not to reject the value of Jewish worship?

3) How might a preacher or catechist emphasize the continuity
between the Christian faith and its Jewish origins?

Chapter 9: John 9:1–41: Fourth Sunday of Lent

1) Should illness be viewed as God's punishment for sin?

2) What is the problem of anti-Jewish bias in this story?

3) How does this passage convey the difference between physical
and spiritual sight?

4) How may the experience of the Johannine community being
expelled from the synagogue relate to this story?

Chapter 10: John 11:1–45: Fifth Sunday of Lent

1) How does the way in which *hoi Ioudaioi* is translated affect the
understanding of this passage?

2) In what ways can preachers and catechists promote an accurate
understanding of *hoi Ioudaioi* in these verses?

3) What roles does weeping play in this story?

Chapter 11: John 3:16–18: Trinity Sunday

See questions in Cycle B: Fourth Sunday of Lent

Chapter 12: John 6:51-58: Most Holy Body and Blood of Christ (Corpus Christi)

> How does this selection differ from the same passage chosen for the Twentieth Sunday of the Year (Cycle B)?

READINGS FROM THE GOSPEL OF JOHN IN CYCLE B

Chapter 13: John 1:6–8, 19–28: Third Sunday of Advent

1) How does the evangelist identify the opponents of Jesus in this section?
2) How should the preacher or catechist be aware of the lack of precision in this description of Jesus' opponents?
3) Are there similarities in those who oppose both Jesus and John the Baptist?

Chapter 14: John 2:13–25: Third Sunday of Lent

1) How does John's version of this account differ from the Synoptic gospels?
2) Did the Johannine community's understanding of the Temple worship impact the way this passage was written?
3) What are the various ways in understanding Jesus "cleansing the temple"?
4) What are the implications of these understandings for preachers and catechists?
5) Is there a sense of anachronism in the evangelist's account?

Chapter 15: John 3:14–21: Fourth Sunday of Lent

1) What role does the story of Moses lifting up a bronze serpent play in this story?
2) How is dualism present in this account?
3) How may preachers and catechists make use of a positive parallel between Moses and Jesus?

Chapter 16: John 12:12–16: Palm Sunday of the Lord's Passion

1) How is understanding the role of crowds important in this section?
2) In what ways may preachers and catechists present the triumphal entry of Jesus into Jerusalem?

Chapter 17: John 6:24–35: Eighteenth Sunday of the Year

1) What occurs in the dialogue between Jesus and the crowd?
2) What is the significance of receiving bread from heaven as a sign?
3) In what specific ways may preachers and catechists approach this text?

Chapter 18: John 6:41–51: Nineteenth Sunday of the Year

1) What is the change in identity of Jesus' opponents?
2) How does the different setting affect the references to *hoi Ioudaioi*?

Chapter 19: John 6:51–58: Twentieth Sunday of the Year

See questions in Cycle B: Nineteenth Sunday of the Year

Chapter 20: John 18:33–37: Christ the King

See questions in Cycle A: Good Friday

Chapter 21: John 19:31–37: Most Sacred Heart of Jesus

See questions in Cycle A: Good Friday

Chapter 22: John 6:51–59; 11:17–27; 11:32–45: All Souls

See questions in Cycle B: Nineteenth Sunday of the Year and Cycle A: Fifth Sunday of Lent

Chapter 23: John 2:13–22: Dedication of the Lateran Basilica

See questions in Cycle B: Third Sunday of Lent

READINGS FROM THE GOSPEL OF JOHN IN CYCLE C

Chapter 24: John 2:1–11: Second Sunday of the Year

1) What are some of the important features of Judaism presented by John in this story?
2) How is this passage indicative of Jesus replacing Jewish practices and views?
3) How may preachers and catechists use the image of "new wine"?

Chapter 25: John 8:1–11: Fifth Sunday of Lent

1) What is unique about this Gospel narrative?
2) What role do witnesses play in this story?
3) What is the importance of Mosaic Law?
4) What is the significance of Jesus' opponents in this incident?
5) How may preachers and catechists present the meaning of this passage?

List of Jewish Terms and Sources

1. **Aboth**—Sometimes known as **Pirke Aboth**, this tract in the Mishnah is a collection of ethical reflections by sages concerned with life lived in accordance with the Law, usually framed in maxims and memorable sayings.

2. **Bab Adodah Zorah**—This tract in the Talmud gives laws regarding idolatry and those who worship false gods.

3. **Baba Bathra**—This tract in the Mishnah regards the rights and obligations between individuals and communities, in particular relationship to contracts and written agreements.

4. **Baba Kava**—This tract in the Talmud treats of damages for physical injuries.

5. **Berakoth**—This tract in the Mishnah outlines the daily prayer and liturgical acts required of Jews, with emphasis on the form of prayer known as a *berakah* or blessing.

6. **Betzah (or Yom Tob)**—This tract in the Mishnah regards the preparation and management of foods, especially spices, for festival days.

7. **Cairo Genizah**—The word *genizah* refers to a special storage room in synagogues in which worn copies of sacred books and other blessed objects are kept until buried or otherwise disposed of. The synagogue in Cairo (882 CE) contained an immense treasure of such texts and it is from the Cairo *genizah* that copies of ancient liturgies, books of the Bible, poetry, and other Hebrew works long thought to be lost were rediscovered around 1896 CE.

8. **Haggadah**—These parts of the Mishnah and the Talmud regard nonlegal matters such as moral teaching, dreams, stories, speculative theological notions, and the like, frequently presented in the context of biblical exegesis.

9. **Hannukah** (Feast of the Dedication of the Temple)—The festival of Hannukah remembers the cleansing of the Temple from Syrian domination in the year 165 BCE. A cruse of oil that was not profaned by the Syrian invaders stayed lit miraculously for eight days, marking the rededication of the Temple to God.

10. **Kelim**—This tract in the Mishnah deals with the cleanliness of vessels.

11. **Ketuboth**—This tract in the Mishnah deals with marriage contracts, covering the financial commitments of husband and wife, especially that of the dowry.

12. **Kilaim**—This tract in the Mishnah deals with prohibitions in the Bible on the combining of certain seeds, trees, fabrics, and even the mixed breeding of animals.

13. **Midrash**—this is a branch of Oral Law (eventually written down) that expounds on the legal parts of the scriptures not otherwise described in any detail in the Bible. Midrashim (the plural of Midrash) are divided into two kinds: (1) those that deal with the Mosaic Law and (2) those that reflect on nonlegal aspects of Jewish life in the scriptures as found in stories, sermons, fables, ethical sayings, and the like. This second category is known as *Haggadah*.

14. **Mishnah**—This is the compilation of early oral laws in Judaism, dating from approximately 200 CE. The Mishnah is cited in *The Gospel of John Set Free* only as a source for understanding what was probably taught and practiced in the time of Jesus. The Mishnah is divided into six books or "orders" that describe how Jewish life is to be lived: (1) *Zeraim* (on blessings and agricultural laws); (2) *Moed* (on the Sabbath and holy days); (3) *Nashim* (on marriage, divorce, and promise making); (4) *Nezikin* (on civil law, damages for injuries, idolatry, and also includes the *Pirke Aboth* or ethical sayings of

rabbis); (5) *Kodashim* (on Temple sacrifices and dietary laws); and (6) *Tohoroth* (on ritual cleanliness and purity).

15. **Niddah**—This tract in the Mishnah deals with menstruation.

16. **Passover**—This is a pilgrim feast in Exodus 23:14, remembering the birth of the Israelite nation and God's deliverance of Israel from Egyptian bondage (Lev 23ff.). The liberating event of the Passover was commemorated by the offering of the paschal lamb in the Temple and the obligation of eating unleavened bread or *matzah*.

17. **Peah**—This tract in the Mishnah deals with gifts and tithes for the poor, often in agricultural produce.

18. **Qumran**—This is the name of the location where a series of caves was discovered in approximately 1948, holding a large cache of biblical and other manuscripts from what was known as the Essene community of Jews, who lived in the desert outside Jerusalem in the first century CE and awaited the Messiah according to many unique doctrines.

19. **Rosh ha-Shanah**—This tract in the Mishnah regards the sanctification of the new moon and the Rosh ha-Shanah liturgy; also the name of a four-day festival that celebrates the Jewish new year.

20. **Sanhedrin**—This tract in the Mishnah regards the procedures to be followed in civil, criminal, and religious law courts. It is also the name of the Jewish law court that exercised supreme religious, judicial, and legislative authority in Palestine during the first century CE.

21. **Shabbath**—(1) This tract in the Mishnah deals with the observance of the Sabbath; (2) Exodus 20:8–11 refers to the *Shabbath* as a weekly celebration to be remembered and kept holy by refraining from toil and labor. The *Shabbath* is a day set aside for spiritual and moral regeneration.

22. **Shemoth Rabba**—This is the Haggadah Midrash on the Book of Exodus.

23. **Sotah**—This tract in the Mishnah deals with the treatment of a woman caught in the act of adultery.

24. **Tabernacles (Sukkot)**—Leviticus 23:42 indicates that the feast of Tabernacles should be celebrated for seven days and that "you shall live in booths for seven days." The rabbis pointed out that to live in booths or sukkot is a demonstration of Jewish faith in God and God's miracle on behalf of the Jewish people.

25. **Talmud**—This is a compilation of the Mishnah and the Gemara (commentary or discussion on the Mishnah). Two main forms of the Talmud are the *Babylonian Talmud* and the *Palestinian Talmud,* both from approximately the fifth century CE.

26. **Tillin**—This Midrash comments on the psalms.

27. **Tosefta**—This collection of Jewish oral traditions is similar to but not a part of the Mishnah; arranged in tracts like those of the Mishnah, it contains a substantial amount of Haggadah material over that found in the Mishnah.

28.**Tosefta Shabbath**—This tract in the Tosefta describes the observance and meaning of the Sabbath.

29. **Tosefta Shekalim**—This tract in the Tosefta deals with oath taking and freewill offerings for religious acts.

Chart of Readings from the Gospel of John in This Volume

PAGE	GOSPEL CITATION	CYCLE AND FEAST	STORY
27	John 1:1–18	A, B, C: Christmas	Prologue of John's Gospel
95	John 1:6–8, 19–28	B: Third Sunday of Advent	Prologue of John's Gospel
127	John 2:1–11	C: Second Sunday of the Year (Ordinary Time)	Wedding Feast at Cana
98	John 2:13–25	B: Third Sunday of Lent	Cleansing of the Temple
104	John 3:14–21	B: Fourth Sunday of Lent	The Bronze Serpent and Those Who Live in Light
90	John 3:16–18	A: Trinity Sunday	The Bronze Serpent and Those Who Live in Light
112	John 6:24–35	B: Eighteenth Sunday of the Year (Ordinary Time)	Bread of Life Discourse (Part One)
117	John 6:41–51	B: Nineteenth Sunday of the Year (Ordinary Time)	Bread of Life Discourse (Part Two)

PAGE	GOSPEL CITATION	CYCLE AND FEAST	STORY
91	John 6:51–58	A: Most Holy Body and Blood of Christ (Corpus Christi)	Bread of Life Discourse (Part Three)
134	John 8:1–11	C: Fifth Sunday of Lent	Woman Caught in Adultery
78	John 9:1–41	A: Fourth Sunday of Lent	Cure of the Man Born Blind
85	John 11:1–45	A: Fifth Sunday of Lent	Raising of Lazarus
108	John 12:12–16	B: Palm Sunday of the Lord's Passion	Entrance into Jerusalem
32	John 13:1–15	A, B, C: Holy Thursday	The Washing of the Feet at the Last Supper
36	John 18:1—19:42	A, B, C: Good Friday	The Passion and Death of Jesus
120	John 18:33–37	B: Christ the King	Excerpt from the Passion
68	John 20:19–23	A, B, C: Pentecost Sunday	The Unbelief of Thomas; Bestowal of the Spirit
61	John 20:19–31	A, B, C: Second Sunday of Easter	The Unbelief of Thomas after the Resurrection

Suggested Reading

(* denotes works cited in the text)

ECCLESIAL DOCUMENTS

**God's Mercy Endures Forever: Guidelines on the Presentation of Jews and Judaism in Catholic Preaching*. Bishops' Committee on the Liturgy, National Conference of Catholic Bishops. Washington: United States Catholic Conference, 1988.

*"Guidelines and Suggestions for Implementing the Conciliar Declaration, *Nostra Aetate (n. 4)*." Vatican Commission for Religious Relations with the Jews. January 1975. In *Stepping Stones to Jewish Christian Relations: An Unabridged Collection of Christian Documents,* edited by H. Croner, 11–16. London: Stimulus Books, 1977. (See Appendix I to the present volume, pp. 157–65, for this document in its entirety, courtesy of www. vatican.va.)

*"An Instruction on the Historical Truth of the Gospels." Pontifical Biblical Commission. In *A Christological Catechism: New Testament Answers,* by Joseph A. Fitzmyer, 131–42. New York: Paulist Press, 1982.

*"The Jewish People and Their Sacred Scriptures in the Christian Bible." Pontifical Biblical Commission. Rome: Vatican Press, 2001.

* *Nostra Aetate*. In *The Documents of Vatican II,* edited by Walter M. Abbott, 660–71. New York: Guild Press, 1966.

*"Notes on the Correct Way to Present the Jews and Judaism in Preaching and Catechesis in the Roman Catholic Church."

Vatican Commission for Religious Relations with the Jews. *Origins* 15/7 (July 4, 1985), 102–7. (See Appendix II to the present volume, pp. 167–80, for this document in its entirety, courtesy of www.vatican.va.)

BOOKS AND ARTICLES

Ashton, J. "The Identity and Function of the *Ioudaioi* in the Fourth Gospel." *Novum Testamentum* 27 (1985): 40–75.

Beck, Norman A. *Mature Christianity: The Recognition and Repudiation of the Anti-Jewish Polemic of the New Testament.* Selinsgrove, PA: Susquehanna University Press, 1985.

Boys, Mary C. *Has God Only One Blessing?: Judaism as a Source of Christian Self-Understanding.* New York: Paulist Press, 2000.

Brown, R. E. *The Gospel According to John* (Anchor Bible 29–29a). Garden City, NY: Doubleday, 1966–70.

————. *The Community of the Beloved Disciple.* New York: Paulist Press, 1979.

Epp, E. J. "Anti-Semitism and the Popularity of the Fourth Gospel." *CCAR Journal* 22 (1975): 35–57.

Granskou, D. "Anti-Judaism in the Passion Accounts of the Fourth Gospel." In *Anti-Judaism in Early Christianity.* Vol. 1, *Paul and the Gospels,* edited by P. Richardson, 201–16. Waterloo, Ontario: Wilfrid Laurier University, 1986.

Kysar, Robert. "Anti-Semitism in the Gospel of John." In *Faith and Polemic: Studies in Anti-Semitism and Early Christianity,* edited by Craig A. Evans and Donald A. Hanger. Minneapolis: Fortress Press, 1993.

Martyn, J. L. *History and Theology in the Fourth Gospel,* 2nd ed. Nashville, TN: Abingdon, 1979.

Mussner, Franz. *Tractate on the Jews*. Philadelphia: Fortress, 1984.

*Sanders, E. P. *Jesus and Judaism*. Philadelphia: Fortress, 1985.

Sloyan, Gerald S. *What Are They Saying About John?* New York: Paulist Press, 2006.

Smiga, G. *Pain and Polemic: Anti-Judaism in the Gospels,* 134–73. New York: Paulist Press, 1992.

Smith, D. M. "Judaism and the Gospel of John." In *Jews and Christians: Exploring the Past, Present, and Future,* edited by J. H. Charlesworth, 76–96. New York: Crossroad, 1990.

Townsend, J. T. "The Gospel of John and the Jews: The Story of a Religious Divorce." In *Antisemitism and the Foundations of Christianity,* edited by A. Davies, 72–79. New York: Paulist Press, 1979.

von Wahlde, U. C. "The Johannine 'Jews': A Critical Survey." *New Testament Studies* 28 (1982): 33–60.

————· "The Gospel of John and the Presentation of Jews and Judaism." In *Within Context: Essays on Jews and Judaism in the New Testament,* edited by David Efroymson, Eugene Fisher, and Leon Klenicki, 67–84. Collegeville, MN: Liturgical Press, 1993.

Appendix I:
Commission for Religious Relations with the Jews "Guidelines and Suggestions for Implementing the Conciliar Declaration, *Nostra Aetate* (n. 4)"

INTRODUCTORY NOTE

The document is published over the signature of Cardinal Willebrands, in his capacity as President of the new Commission for the Catholic Church's religious relations with the Jews, instituted by Paul VI on 22 October 1974. It comes out a short time after the ninth anniversary of the promulgation of *Nostra Aetate,* the Second Vatican Council's Declaration on the Church's relations with non-Christian religions.

The "Guidelines and Suggestions", which refer to n. 4 of the Declaration, are notable for their almost exclusively practical nature and for their sobriety.

This deliberately practical nature of the text is justified by the fact that it concerns a pragmatic document.

It does not propose a Christian theology of Judaism. Such a theology certainly has an interest for specialist research and reflection, but it still needs considerable study. The new Commission for Religious Relations with the Jews should be able to play a part in the gradual fruition of this endeavor.

The first part of the Document recalls the principal teachings of the Council on the condemnation of anti-Semitism and of all discrimination, and the obligation of reciprocal understanding and of renewed mutual esteem. It also hopes for a better knowledge on the part of Christians of the essence of the religious tradition of Judaism and of the manner in which Jews identify themselves.

The text then proposes a series of concrete suggestions.

The section dedicated to dialogue calls for fraternal dialogue and the establishment of deep doctrinal research. Prayer in common is also proposed as a means of encounter.

With regard to the liturgy, mention is made of the links between the Christian liturgy and the Jewish liturgy and of the caution which is needed in dealing with commentaries on biblical texts, and with liturgical explanations and translations.

The part concerning teaching and education allows the relations between the two Testaments to be made clear. The question of the trial and death of Jesus is also touched upon and stress is laid on the note of expectation which characterizes both the Jewish and the Christian religion. Specialists are invited to conduct serious research and the establishment of chairs of Hebrew studies is encouraged where it is possible, as well as collaboration with Jewish scholars.

The final section deals with the possibilities of common social action in the context of a search for social justice and for peace.

The conclusion touches on, among other things, the ecumenical aspect of the problem of relations with Judaism, the initiatives of local churches in this area, and the essential lines of the mission of the new Commission instituted by the Holy See.

The great sobriety of the text is noted also in the concrete suggestions which it puts forward. But it would certainly be wrong to interpret such sobriety as being indicative of a limiting program of activities. The document does propose limited suggestions for some key sectors, but it is a document meant for the universal Church, and as such it cannot take account of all the individual situations. The suggestions put forward are intended to give ideas to those who were asking themselves how to start on a local level that dialogue which the text invites them to begin and to develop. These suggestions are mentioned because of their value as examples. They are made because it seems that they could find ample application and that their proposal at the same time constitutes an apt program for aiding local churches to organize their own activities, in order to harmonize with the general movement of the universal Church in dialogue with Judaism.

The Document can be considered from a certain point of view as the Commission's first step for the realization of religious relations with Judaism. It will devolve on the new Commission to prepare and put forward, when necessary, the further developments which may seem necessary in order that the initiative of the Second Vatican Council in this important area may continue to bear fruit on a local and on a worldwide level, for the benefit of peace of heart and harmony of spirit of all who work under the protection of the one Almighty God.

The Document, which gives the invitation to an effort of mutual understanding and collaboration, coincides with the opening of the Holy Year, which is consecrated to the theme of reconciliation. It is impossible not to perceive in such a coincidence an invitation to study and to apply in concrete terms throughout the whole world the suggestions which the Document proposes. Likewise one cannot fail to hope that our Jewish brothers too may find in it useful indications for their participation in a commitment which is common.

PREAMBLE

The Declaration *Nostra Aetate,* issued by the Second Vatican Council on 28 October 1965, "on the relationship of the Church to non-Christian religions" (n. 4), marks an important milestone in the history of Jewish-Christian relations.

Moreover, the step taken by the Council finds its historical setting in circumstances deeply affected by the memory of the persecution and massacre of Jews which took place in Europe just before and during the Second World War.

Although Christianity sprang from Judaism, taking from it certain essential elements of its faith and divine cult, the gap dividing them was deepened more and more, to such an extent that Christian and Jew hardly knew each other.

After two thousand years, too often marked by mutual ignorance and frequent confrontation, the Declaration *Nostra Aetate* provides an opportunity to open or to continue a dialogue with a view to better mutual understanding. Over the past nine years, many steps in this direction have been taken in various countries. As a result, it is easier to distinguish the conditions under which a new relationship between Jews and Christians may be worked out and developed. This seems the right moment to propose, following the guidelines of the Council, some concrete suggestions born of experience, hoping that they will help to bring into actual existence in the life of the Church the intentions expressed in the conciliar document.

While referring the reader back to this document, we may simply restate here that the spiritual bonds and historical links binding the Church to Judaism condemn (as opposed to the very spirit of Christianity) all forms of anti-Semitism and discrimination, which in any case the dignity of the human person alone would suffice to condemn. Further still, these links and relationships render obligatory a better mutual understanding and renewed mutual esteem. On the practical level in particular, Christians must therefore strive to acquire a better knowledge of the basic components of the religious tradition of Judaism; they must strive to learn by what essential traits the Jews define themselves in the light of their own religious experience.

With due respect for such matters of principle, we simply propose some first practical applications in different essential areas of the Church's life, with a view to launching or developing sound relations between Catholics and their Jewish brothers.

I. DIALOGUE

To tell the truth, such relations as there have been between Jew and Christian have scarcely ever risen above the level of monologue. From now on, real dialogue must be established. Dialogue presupposes that each side wishes to know the other, and wishes to increase and deepen its knowledge of the other. It constitutes a particularly suitable means of favoring a better mutual knowledge and, especially in the case of dialogue between Jews and Christians, of probing the riches of one's own tradition. Dialogue demands respect for the other as he is; above all, respect for his faith and his religious convictions.

In virtue of her divine mission, and her very nature, the Church must preach Jesus Christ to the world (*Ad Gentes,* 2). Lest the witness of Catholics to Jesus Christ should give offence to Jews, they must take care to live and spread their Christian faith while maintaining the strictest respect for religious liberty in line with the teaching of the Second Vatican Council (Declaration *Dignitatis Humanae*). They will likewise strive to understand the difficulties which arise for the Jewish soul—rightly imbued with an extremely high, pure notion of the divine transcendence when faced with the mystery of the incarnate Word.

While it is true that a widespread air of suspicion, inspired by an unfortunate past, is still dominant in this particular area, Christians, for their part, will be able to see to what extent the responsibility is theirs and deduce practical conclusions for the future.

In addition to friendly talks, competent people will be encouraged to meet and to study together the many problems deriving from the fundamental convictions of Judaism and of Christianity. In order not to hurt (even involuntarily) those taking part, it will be vital to guarantee, not only tact, but a great openness of spirit and diffidence with respect to one's own prejudices.

In whatever circumstances as shall prove possible and mutually acceptable, one might encourage a common meeting in the presence of God, in prayer and silent meditation, a highly efficacious way of finding that humility, that openness of heart and mind, necessary prerequisites for a deep knowledge of oneself and of others. In particular, that will be done in connection with great causes such as the struggle for peace and justice.

II. LITURGY

The existing links between the Christian liturgy and the Jewish liturgy will be borne in mind. The idea of a living community in the service of God, and in the service of men for the love of God, such as it is realized in the liturgy, is just as characteristic of the Jewish liturgy as it is of the Christian one. To improve Jewish-Christian relations, it is important to take cognizance of those common elements of the liturgical life (formulas, feasts, rites, etc.) in which the Bible holds an essential place.

An effort will be made to acquire a better understanding of whatever in the Old Testament retains its own perpetual value (cf. *Dei Verbum,* 14–15), since that has not been cancelled by the later interpretation of the New Testament. Rather, the New Testament brings out the full meaning of the Old, while both Old and New illumine and explain each other (cf. *ibid.* 16). This is all the more important since liturgical reform is now bringing the text of the Old Testament ever more frequently to the attention of Christians.

When commenting on biblical texts, emphasis will be laid on the continuity of our faith with that of the earlier Covenant, in the perspective of the promises, without minimizing those elements of Christianity which are original. We believe that those promises were fulfilled with the first coming of Christ. But it is none the less true that we still await their perfect fulfillment in his glorious return at the end of time.

With respect to liturgical readings, care will be taken to see that homilies based on them will not distort their meaning, especially when it is a question of passages which seem to show the Jewish people as such in an unfavorable light. Efforts will be made so to instruct the Christian people that they will understand the true interpretation of all the texts and their meaning for the contemporary believer.

Commissions entrusted with the task of liturgical translation will pay particular attention to the way in which they express those phrases and passages which Christians, if not well informed, might misunderstand because of prejudice. Obviously, one cannot alter the text of the Bible. The point is that, with a version destined for liturgical use, there should be an overriding preoccupation to bring out explicitly the meaning of a text,* while taking scriptural studies into account.

The preceding remarks also apply to introductions to biblical readings, to the Prayer of the Faithful, and to commentaries printed in missals used by the laity.

III. TEACHING AND EDUCATION

Although there is still a great deal of work to be done, a better understanding of Judaism itself and its relationship to Christianity has been achieved in recent years thanks to the teaching of the Church, the study and research of scholars, as also to the beginning of dialogue. In this respect, the following facts deserve to be recalled.

- It is the same God, "inspirer and author of the books of both Testaments", (*Dei Verbum,* 16), who speaks both in the old and new Covenants.
- Judaism in the time of Christ and the Apostles was a complex reality, embracing many different trends, many spiritual, religious, social and cultural values.
- The Old Testament and the Jewish tradition founded upon it must not be set against the New Testament in such a way that

the former seems to constitute a religion of only justice, fear and legalism, with no appeal to the love of God and neighbor (cf. Deut 6:5, Lev 19:18, Matt 22:34–40).

- Jesus was born of the Jewish people, as were his Apostles and a large number of his first disciples. When he revealed himself as the Messiah and Son of God (cf. Matt 16:16), the bearer of the new Gospel message, he did so as the fulfillment and perfection of the earlier Revelation. And, although his teaching had a profoundly new character, Christ, nevertheless, in many instances, took his stand on the teaching of the Old Testament. The New Testament is profoundly marked by its relation to the Old. As the Second Vatican Council declared: "God, the inspirer and author of the books of both Testaments, wisely arranged that the New Testament be hidden in the Old and the Old be made manifest in the New" (*Dei Verbum,* 16). Jesus also used teaching methods similar to those employed by the rabbis of his time.

- With regard to the trial and death of Jesus, the Council recalled that "what happened in his passion cannot be blamed upon all the Jews then living, without distinction, nor upon the Jews of today" (*Nostra Aetate,* 4).

- The history of Judaism did not end with the destruction of Jerusalem, but rather went on to develop a religious tradition. And, although we believe that the importance and meaning of that tradition were deeply affected by the coming of Christ, it is still nonetheless rich in religious values.

- With the prophets and the apostle Paul, "the Church awaits the day, known to God alone, on which all peoples will address the Lord in a single voice and 'serve him with one accord' (Soph 3:9)" (*Nostra Aetate,* 4).

Information concerning these questions is important at all levels of Christian instruction and education. Among sources of information, special attention should be paid to the following:

- catechisms and religious textbooks;
- history books;
- the mass-media (press, radio, cinema, television).

The effective use of these means presupposes the thorough formation of instructors and educators in training schools, seminaries and universities.

Research into the problems bearing on Judaism and Jewish-Christian relations will be encouraged among specialists, particularly in the fields of exegesis, theology, history and sociology. Higher institutions of Catholic research, in association if possible with other similar Christian institutions and experts, are invited to contribute to the solution of such problems. Wherever possible, chairs of Jewish studies will be created, and collaboration with Jewish scholars encouraged.

IV. JOINT SOCIAL ACTION

Jewish and Christian tradition, founded on the Word of God, is aware of the value of the human person, the image of God. Love of the same God must show itself in effective action for the good of mankind.

In the spirit of the prophets, Jews and Christians will work willingly together, seeking social justice and peace at every level—local, national and international. At the same time, such collaboration can do much to foster mutual understanding and esteem.

CONCLUSION

The Second Vatican Council has pointed out the path to follow in promoting deep fellowship between Jews and Christians. But there is still a long road ahead. The problem of Jewish-Christian relations concerns the Church as such, since it is when "pondering her own mystery" that she encounters the mystery of Israel. Therefore, even in areas where no Jewish communities exist, this remains an important problem. There is also an ecumenical aspect to the question: the very return of Christians to the sources and origins of their faith, grafted on to the earlier Covenant, helps the search for unity in Christ, the cornerstone.

In this field, the bishops will know what best to do on the pastoral level, within the general disciplinary framework of the Church and in line with the common teaching of her magisterium. For example, they will create some suitable commissions or secretariats on a national or regional level, or appoint some competent person to promote the implementation of the conciliar directives and the suggestions made above.

On 22 October 1974, the Holy Father instituted for the universal Church this Commission for Religious Relations with the Jews, joined to the Secretariat for Promoting Christian Unity. This special Commission, created to encourage and foster religious relations between Jews and Catholics — and to do so eventually in collaboration with other Christians — will be, within the limits of its competence, at the service of all interested organizations, providing information for them, and helping them to pursue their task in conformity with the instructions of the Holy See.

The Commission wishes to develop this collaboration in order to implement, correctly and effectively, the express intentions of the Council.

Given at Rome, 1 December 1974.

Johannes Card. Willebrands
President of the Commission

Pierre-Marie de Contenson, O.P.
Secretary of the Commission

---

*Thus the formula "the Jews", in St. John, sometimes according to the context means "the leaders of the Jews", or "the adversaries of Jesus", terms which express better the thought of the evangelist and avoid appearing to arraign the Jewish people as such. Another example is the use of the words "pharisee" and "pharisaism" which have taken on a largely pejorative meaning.

Appendix II:
Commission for Religious Relations with the Jews
"Notes on the Correct Way to Present the Jews and Judaism in Preaching and Catechesis in the Roman Catholic Church"

PRELIMINARY CONSIDERATIONS

On March 6th, 1982, Pope John Paul II told delegates of Episcopal conferences and other experts, meeting in Rome to study relations between the Church and Judaism:

> " '[Y]ou yourselves were concerned, during your sessions, with Catholic teaching and catechesis regarding Jews and Judaism.' We should aim, in this field, that Catholic teaching at its different levels, in catechesis to children and young people, presents Jews and Judaism, not only in an honest and objective manner, free from prejudices and without any offences, but also with full awareness of the heritage common" to Jews and Christians.

In this passage, so charged with meaning, the Holy Father plainly drew inspiration from the Council Declaration *Nostra Aetate,* 4, which says:

> "All should take pains, then, lest in catechetical instruction and in the preaching of God's Word they teach anything out of harmony with the truth of the Gospel and the spirit

of Christ"; as also from these words: "Since the spiritual patrimony common to Christians and Jews is thus so great, this sacred Synod wishes to foster and recommend mutual understanding and respect."

In the same way, the *Guidelines and Suggestions for Implementing the Conciliar Declaration Nostra Aetate* (4) ends its chapter III, entitled "Teaching and education", which lists a number of practical things to be done, with this recommendation:

"Information concerning these questions is important at all levels of Christian instruction and education. Among sources of information, special attention should be paid to the following:

- catechisms and religious textbooks;
- history books;
- the mass media (press, radio, cinema, television).

The effective use of these means presupposes the thorough formation of instructors and educators in training schools, seminaries and universities" (*AAS* 77, 1975, p. 73).

The paragraphs which follow are intended to serve this purpose.

I. RELIGIOUS TEACHING AND JUDAISM

1. In *Nostra Aetate* 4, the Council speaks of the "spiritual bonds linking" Jews and Christians and of the "great spiritual patrimony" common to both and it further asserts that "the Church of Christ acknowledges that, according to the mystery of God's saving design, the beginning of her faith and her election are already found among the patriarchs, Moses and the prophets".

2. Because of the unique relations that exist between Christianity and Judaism—"linked together at the very level of their identity" (John Paul II, 6th March, 1982)—relations "founded on the design of the God of the Covenant" *(ibid.)*, the Jews and Judaism should not occupy an occasional and marginal place in catechesis: their presence there is essential and should be organically integrated.

3. This concern for Judaism in Catholic teaching has not merely a historical or archeological foundation. As the Holy Father said in the speech already quoted, after he had again mentioned the "common patrimony" of the Church and Judaism as "considerable": "To assess it carefully in itself and with due awareness of the faith and religious life of the Jewish people *as they are professed and practiced still today*, can greatly help us to understand better certain aspects of the life of the Church" (italics added). It is a question then of *pastoral* concern for a still living reality closely related to the Church. The Holy Father has stated this permanent reality of the Jewish people in a remarkable theological formula, in his allocution to the Jewish community of West Germany at Mainz, on November 17th, 1980: "the people of God of the Old Covenant, which has never been revoked".

4. Here we should recall the passage in which the *Guidelines and Suggestions* (I) tried to define the fundamental condition of dialogue: "respect for the other as he is", knowledge of the "basic components of the religious traditions of Judaism" and again learning "by what essential trait the Jews define themselves in the light of their own religious experience" (Introd.).

5. The singular character and the difficulty of Christian teaching about Jews and Judaism lies in this, that it needs to balance a number of pairs of ideas which express the relation between the two economies of the Old and New Testament:

- Promise and Fulfillment
- Continuity and Newness
- Singularity and Universality
- Uniqueness and Exemplary Nature.

This means that the theologian and the catechist who deals with the subject needs to show in his practice of teaching that:

- promise and fulfillment throw light on each other;
- newness lies in a metamorphosis of what was there before;
- the singularity of the people of the Old Testament is not exclusive and is open, in the divine vision, to a universal extension;
- the uniqueness of the Jewish people is meant to have the force of an example.

6. Finally, "work that is of poor quality and lacking in precision would be extremely detrimental" to Judaeo-Christian dialogue (John Paul II, speech of March 6th, 1982). But it would be above all detrimental — since we are talking of teaching and education — to Christian identity *(ibid)*.

7. "In virtue of her divine mission, the Church" which is to be "the all-embracing means of salvation" in which alone "the fullness of the means of salvation can be obtained" *(Unit. Red. 3)* "must of her nature proclaim Jesus Christ to the world" (cf. *Guidelines and Suggestions*, I). Indeed we believe that it is through him that we go to the Father (cf. Jn 14:6) "and this is eternal life, that they know thee the only true God and Jesus Christ whom thou hast sent" (Jn 17:33).

Jesus affirms *(ibid.* 10:16) that "there shall be one flock and one shepherd". Church and Judaism cannot then be seen as two parallel ways of salvation and the Church must witness to Christ as the Redeemer for all, "while maintaining the strictest respect for religious liberty in line with the teaching of the Second Vatican Council (Declaration *Dignitatis Humanae)"* *(Guidelines and Suggestions,* I).

8. The urgency and importance of precise, objective and rigorously accurate teaching on Judaism for our faithful follows too from the danger of anti-Semitism which is always ready to reappear under different guises. The question is not merely to uproot from among the faithful the remains of anti-Semitism still to be found here and there, but much rather to arouse in them, through educational work, an exact knowledge of the wholly unique "bond" *(Nostra Aetate,* 4) which joins us as a Church to the Jews and to Judaism. In this way, they would learn to appreciate and love the latter, who have been chosen by God to prepare the coming of Christ and have preserved everything that was progressively revealed and given in the course of that preparation, notwithstanding their difficulty in recognizing in Him their Messiah.

II. RELATIONS BETWEEN THE
OLD* AND NEW TESTAMENT

1. Our aim should be to show the unity of biblical Revelation (O.T. and N.T.) and of the divine plan, before speaking of each historical event, so as to stress that particular events have meaning when

seen in history as a whole—from creation to fulfillment. This history concerns the whole human race and especially believers. Thus the definitive meaning of the election of Israel does not become clear except in the light of the complete fulfillment (Rom 9–11) and election in Jesus Christ is still better understood with reference to the announcement and the promise (cf. Heb 4:1–11).

2. We are dealing with singular happenings which concern a singular nation but are destined, in the sight of God who reveals his purpose, to take on universal and exemplary significance. The aim is moreover to present the events of the Old Testament not as concerning only the Jews but also as touching us personally. Abraham is truly the father of our faith (cf. Rom 4:11–12; Roman Canon: *patriarchae nostri Abrahae*). And it is said (1 Cor 10:1): *"Our* fathers were all under the cloud, and all passed through the sea"*. The patriarchs, prophets and other personalities of the Old Testament have been venerated and always will be venerated as saints in the liturgical tradition of the Oriental Church as also of the Latin Church.

3. From the unity of the divine plan derives the problem of the relation between the Old and New Testaments. The Church already from apostolic times (cf. 1 Cor 10:11; Heb 10:1) and then constantly in tradition resolved this problem by means of typology, which emphasizes the primordial value that the Old Testament must have in the Christian view. Typology however makes many people uneasy and is perhaps the sign of a problem unresolved.

4. Hence in using typology, the teaching and practice of which we have received from the Liturgy and from the Fathers of the Church, we should be careful to avoid any transition from the Old to the New Testament which might seem merely a rupture.

The Church, in the spontaneity of the Spirit which animates her, has vigorously condemned the attitude of Marcion** and always opposed his dualism.

5. It should also be emphasized that typological interpretation consists in reading the Old Testament as preparation and, in certain aspects, outline and foreshadowing of the New (cf. e.g., Heb 5:5–10 etc.). Christ is henceforth the key and point of reference to the Scriptures: the rock was Christ (1 Cor 10:4).

6. It is true then, and should be stressed, that the Church and Christians read the Old Testament in the light of the event of the dead and risen Christ and that on these grounds there is a Christian reading

of the Old Testament which does not necessarily coincide with the Jewish reading. Thus Christian identity and Jewish identity should be carefully distinguished in their respective reading of the Bible.

But this detracts nothing from the value of the Old Testament in the Church and does nothing to hinder Christians from profiting discerningly from the traditions of Jewish reading.

7. Typological reading only manifests the unfathomable riches of the Old Testament, its inexhaustible content and the mystery of which it is full, and should not lead us to forget that it retains its own value as Revelation that the New Testament often does no more than resume (cf. Mk 12:29–31). Moreover, the New Testament itself demands to be read in the light of the Old. Primitive Christian catechesis constantly had recourse to this (cf. e.g., 1 Cor 5:6–8; 10:1–11).

8. Typology further signifies reaching towards the accomplishment of the divine plan, when "God will be all in all" (1 Cor 15:28). This holds true also for the Church which, realized already in Christ, yet awaits its definitive perfecting as the Body of Christ.

The fact that the Body of Christ is still tending towards its full stature (cf. Eph 4:12–19) takes nothing from the value of being a Christian. So also the calling of the patriarchs and the Exodus from Egypt do not lose their importance and value in God's design from being at the same time intermediate stages (cf. e.g., *Nostra Aetate*, 4).

9. The Exodus, for example, represents an experience of salvation and liberation that is not complete in itself, but has in it, over and above its own meaning, the capacity to be developed further. Salvation and liberation are already accomplished in Christ and gradually realized by the sacraments in the Church. This makes way for the fulfillment of God's design, which awaits its final consummation with the return of Jesus as Messiah, for which we pray each day. The Kingdom, for the coming of which we also pray each day, will be finally established. With salvation and liberation the elect and the whole of creation will be transformed in Christ (Rom 8:19–23).

10. Furthermore, in underlining the eschatological dimension of Christianity we shall reach a greater awareness that the people of God of the Old and the New Testament are tending towards a like end in the future: the coming or return of the Messiah—even if they start from two different points of view. It is more clearly understood that the person of the Messiah is not only a point of division for the people of God but also a point of convergence (cf. *Sussidi per l'ecumenismo*

of the diocese of Rome, n. 140). Thus it can be said that Jews and Christians meet in a comparable hope, founded on the same promise made to Abraham (cf. Gen 12:1–3; Heb 6:13–18).

11. Attentive to the same God who has spoken, hanging on the same word, we have to witness to one same memory and one common hope in Him who is the master of history. We must also accept our responsibility to prepare the world for the coming of the Messiah by working together for social justice, respect for the rights of persons and nations and for social and international reconciliation. To this we are driven, Jews and Christians, by the command to love our neighbor, by a common hope for the kingdom of God and by the great heritage of the Prophets. Transmitted soon enough by catechesis, such a conception would teach young Christians in a practical way to cooperate with Jews, going beyond simple dialogue (cf. *Guidelines*, IV).

III. JEWISH ROOTS OF CHRISTIANITY

1. Jesus was and always remained a Jew, his ministry was deliberately limited "to the lost sheep of the house of Israel" (Mt 15:24). Jesus is fully a man of his time, and of his environment—the Jewish Palestinian one of the first century, the anxieties and hopes of which he shared. This cannot but underline both the reality of the Incarnation and the very meaning of the history of salvation, as it has been revealed in the Bible (cf. Rom 1:3–4; Gal 4:4–5).

2. Jesus' relations with biblical law and its more or less traditional interpretations are undoubtedly complex and he showed great liberty towards it (cf. the "antitheses" of the Sermon on the Mount: Mt 5:21–48, bearing in mind the exegetical difficulties; his attitude to rigorous observance of the Sabbath: Mk 3:1–6, etc.).

But there is not doubt that he wished to submit himself to the law (cf. Gal 4:4), that he was circumcised and presented in the Temple like any Jew of his time (cf. Lk 2:21, 22–24), that he was trained in the law's observance. He extolled respect for it (cf. Mt 5:17–20) and invited obedience to it (cf. Mt 8:4). The rhythm of his life was marked by observance of pilgrimages on great feasts, even from his infancy (cf. Lk 2:41–50; Jn 2:13; 7:10, etc.). The importance of the cycle of the Jewish feasts has been frequently underlined in the Gospel of John (cf. 2:13; 5:1; 7:2,10,37; 10:22; 12:1; 18:28; 19:42, etc.).

3. It should be noted also that Jesus often taught in the Synagogues (cf. Mt 4:23: 9:35; Lk 4:15–18; Jn 18:20, etc.) and in the Temple (cf. Jn 18:20, etc.), which he frequented as did the disciples even after the Resurrection (cf. e.g., Acts 2:46; 3:1; 21:26, etc.). He wished to put in the context of synagogue worship the proclamation of his Messiahship (cf. Lk 4:16–21). But above all he wished to achieve the supreme act of the gift of himself in the setting of the domestic liturgy of the Passover or at least of the paschal festivity (cf. Mk 14:1,12 and parallels; Jn 18:28). This also allows of a better understanding of the "memorial" character of the Eucharist.

4. Thus the Son of God is incarnate in a people and a human family (cf. Gal 4:4; Rom 9:5). This takes away nothing, quite the contrary, from the fact that he was born for all men (Jewish shepherds and pagan wise men are found at his crib: Lk 2:8–20; Mt 2:1–12) and died for all men (at the foot of the cross there are Jews, among them Mary and John: Jn 19:25–27, and pagans like the centurion: Mk 15:39 and parallels). Thus he made two peoples one in his flesh (cf. Eph 2:14–17). This explains why with the *Ecclesia ac gentibus* we have, in Palestine and elsewhere, an *Ecclesia ex circumcisione*, of which *Eusebius* for example speaks (H.E. IV, 5).

5. His relations with the Pharisees were not always or wholly polemical. Of this there are many proofs:

- It is Pharisees who warn Jesus of the risks he is running (Lk 13:31);
- Some Pharisees are praised, e.g., "the scribe" of Mk 12:34;
- Jesus eats with Pharisees (Lk 7:36; 14:1).

6. Jesus shares, with the majority of Palestinian Jews of that time, some pharisaic doctrines: the resurrection of the body; forms of piety, like alms-giving, prayer, fasting (cf. Mt 6:1–18) and the liturgical practice of addressing God as Father; the priority of the commandment to love God and our neighbor (cf. Mk 12:28–34). This is so also with Paul (cf. Acts 23:8), who always considered his membership of the Pharisees as a title of honour (cf. *ibid.* 23:6; 26:6; Phil 3:5).

7. Paul also, like Jesus himself, used methods of reading and interpreting Scripture and of teaching his disciples which were common to the Pharisees of their time. This applies to the use of parables

in Jesus' ministry, as also to the method of Jesus and Paul of supporting a conclusion with a quotation from Scripture.

8. It is noteworthy too that the Pharisees are not mentioned in accounts of the Passion. Gamaliel (Acts 5:34–39) defends the apostles in a meeting of the Sanhedrin. An exclusively negative picture of the Pharisees is likely to be inaccurate and unjust (cf. *Guidelines*, Note 1; cf. *AAS*, loc. cit. p. 76). If in the Gospels and elsewhere in the New Testament there are all sorts of unfavorable references to the Pharisees, they should be seen against the background of a complex and diversified movement.

Criticisms of various types of Pharisees are moreover not lacking in rabbinical sources (cf. the *Babylon Talmud*, the *Sotah* treatise 22b, etc.). "Phariseeism" in the pejorative sense can be rife in any religion. It may also be stressed that, if Jesus shows himself severe towards the Pharisees, it is because he is closer to them than to other contemporary Jewish groups (cf. supra n. 17).

9. All this should help us to understand better what St Paul says (Rom 11:16 ff) about the "root" and the "branches". The Church and Christianity, for all their novelty, find their origin in the Jewish milieu of the first century of our era, and more deeply still in the "design of God" (*Nostra Aetate*, 4), realized in the Patriarchs, Moses and the Prophets *(ibid.)*, down to its consummation in Christ Jesus.

IV. THE JEWS IN THE NEW TESTAMENT

1. The *Guidelines* already say (note 1) that "the formula 'the Jews' sometimes, according to the context, means 'the leaders of the Jews' or 'the adversaries of Jesus', terms which express better the thought of the evangelist and avoid appearing to arraign the Jewish people as such". An objective presentation of the role of the Jewish people in the New Testament should take account of these various facts:

A. The Gospels are the outcome of long and complicated editorial work. The dogmatic constitution *Dei Verbum*, following the Pontifical Biblical Commission's Instruction *Sancta Mater Ecclesia*, distinguishes three stages: "The sacred authors wrote the four Gospels, selecting some things from the many which had been handed on by word of mouth or in writing, reducing

some of them to a synthesis, explicating some things in view of
the situation of the Churches, and preserving the form of proclamation, but always in such fashion that they told us the honest
truth about Jesus" (n. 19).

Hence it cannot be ruled out that some references hostile or
less than favorable to the Jews have their historical context in
conflicts between the nascent Church and the Jewish community.

Certain controversies reflect Christian-Jewish relations long
after the time of Jesus.

To establish this is of capital importance if we wish to bring
out the meaning of certain Gospel texts for the Christians of
today.

All this should be taken into account when preparing catechesis and homilies for the last weeks of Lent and Holy Week (cf.
already *Guidelines* II, and now also *Sussidi per l'ecumenismo
nella diocesi di Roma,* 1982, 144 b).

B. It is clear on the other hand that there were conflicts between
Jesus and certain categories of Jews of his time, among them
Pharisees, from the beginning of his ministry (cf. Mk 2:1–11,24;
3:6, etc.).

C. There is moreover the sad fact that the majority of the Jewish
people and its authorities did not believe in Jesus—a fact not
merely of history but of theological bearing, of which St Paul
tries hard to plumb the meaning (Rom chap. 9—11).

D. This fact, accentuated as the Christian mission developed,
especially among the pagans, led inevitably to a rupture between
Judaism and the young Church, now irreducibly separated and
divergent in faith, and this stage of affairs is reflected in the texts
of the New Testament and particularly in the Gospel. There is no
question of playing down or glossing over this rupture; that
could only prejudice the identity of either side.

Nevertheless it certainly does not cancel the spiritual "bond"
of which the Council speaks (*Nostra Aetate,* 4) and which we
propose to dwell on here.

E. Reflecting on this in the light of Scripture, notably of the chapters cited from the epistle to the Romans, Christians should never forget that the faith is a free gift of God (cf. Rom 9:12) and that we should never judge the consciences of others. St Paul's exhortation "do not boast" in your attitude to "the root" (Rom 11:18) has its full point here.

F. There is no putting the Jews who knew Jesus and did not believe in him, or those who opposed the preaching of the apostles, on the same plane with Jews who came after or those of today. If the responsibility of the former remains a mystery hidden with God (cf. Rom 11:25), the latter are in an entirely different situation. Vatican II in the declaration on *Religious Liberty* teaches that "all men are to be immune from coercion" in such wise that in matters religious no one is to be forced to act in a manner contrary to his own beliefs. Nor "restrained from acting in accordance with his own beliefs" (n. 2). This is one of the bases — proclaimed by the Council — on which Judaeo-Christian dialogue rests.

2. The delicate question of responsibility for the death of Christ must be looked at from the standpoint of the conciliar declaration *Nostra Aetate*, 4 and of *Guidelines and Suggestions* (III): "What happened in (Christ's) passion cannot be blamed upon all the Jews then living without distinction nor upon the Jews of today", especially since "authorities of the Jews and those who followed their lead pressed for the death of Christ". Again, further on: "Christ in his boundless love freely underwent his passion and death because of the sins of all men, so that all might attain salvation" (*Nostra Aetate, 4*). The *Catechism* of the Council of Trent teaches that Christian sinners are more to blame for the death of Christ than those few Jews who brought it about — they indeed "knew not what they did" (cf. Lk 23:24) and we know it only too well (Pars I, caput V, Quaest, XI). In the same way and for the same reason, "the Jews should not be presented as repudiated or cursed by God, as if such views followed from the holy Scriptures" (*Nostra Aetate, 4*), even though it is true that "the Church is the new people of God" *(ibid.).*

V. THE LITURGY

1. Jews and Christians find in the Bible the very substance of their liturgy: for the proclamation of God's word, response to it, prayer of praise and intercession for the living and the dead, recourse to the divine mercy. The Liturgy of the word in its own structure originates in Judaism. The prayer of Hours and other liturgical texts and formularies have their parallels in Judaism as do the very formulas of our most venerable prayers, among them the Our Father. The eucharistic prayers also draw inspiration from models in the Jewish tradition. As John Paul II said (Allocution of March 6th, 1982): "the faith and religious life of the Jewish people as they are professed and practiced still today, can greatly help us to understand better certain aspects of the life of the Church. Such is the case of liturgy".

2. This is particularly evident in the great feasts of the liturgical year, like the Passover. Christians and Jews celebrate the Passover: the Jews, the historic Passover looking towards the future; the Christians, the Passover accomplished in the death and resurrection of Christ, although still in expectation of the final consummation (cf. supra n. 9). It is still the "memorial" which comes to us from the Jewish tradition, with a specific content different in each case. On either side, however, there is a like dynamism: for Christians it gives meaning to the eucharistic celebration (cf. the antiphon *O sacrum convivium*), a paschal celebration and as such a making present of the past, but experienced in the expectation of what is to come.

VI. JUDAISM AND CHRISTIANITY IN HISTORY

1. The history of Israel did not end in 70 A.D. (cf. *Guidelines*, II). It continued, especially in a numerous Diaspora which allowed Israel to carry to the whole world a witness — often heroic — of its fidelity to the one God and to "exalt him in the presence of all the living" (Tobit 13:4), while preserving the memory of the land of their forefathers at the hearts of their hope (Passover *Seder*).

Christians are invited to understand this religious attachment which finds its roots in Biblical tradition, without however making their own any particular religious interpretation of this relationship (cf. *Declaration* of the US Conference of Catholic Bishops, November 20, 1975).

The existence of the State of Israel and its political options should be envisaged not in a perspective which is in itself religious, but in their reference to the common principles of international law.

The permanence of Israel (while so many ancient peoples have disappeared without trace) is a historic fact and a sign to be interpreted within God's design. We must in any case rid ourselves of the traditional idea of a people *punished*, preserved as a *living argument* for Christian apologetic. It remains a chosen people, "the pure olive on which were grafted the branches of the wild olive which are the gentiles" (John Paul II, 6th March, 1982, alluding to Rom 11:17–24). We must remember how much the balance of relations between Jews and Christians over two thousand years has been negative. We must remind ourselves how the permanence of Israel is accompanied by a continuous spiritual fecundity, in the rabbinical period, in the Middle Ages and in modern times, taking its start from a patrimony which we long shared, so much so that "the faith and religious life of the Jewish people as they are professed and practiced still today, can greatly help us to understand better certain aspects of the life of the Church" (John Paul II, March 6th, 1982). Catechesis should on the other hand help in understanding the meaning for the Jews of the extermination during the years 1939–1945, and its consequences.

2. Education and catechesis should concern themselves with the problem of racism, still active in different forms of anti-Semitism. The Council presented it thus: "Moreover, (the Church) mindful of her common patrimony with the Jews and motivated by the Gospel's spiritual love and by no political considerations, deplores the hatred, persecutions and displays of anti-Semitism directed against the Jews at any time and from any source" (*Nostra Aetate*, 4). The *Guidelines* comment: "the spiritual bonds and historical links binding the Church to Judaism condemn (as opposed to the very spirit of Christianity) all forms of anti-Semitism and discrimination, which in any case the dignity of the human person alone would suffice to condemn" (*Guidelines*, Preamble).

CONCLUSION

Religious teaching, catechesis and preaching should be a preparation not only for objectivity, justice, tolerance but also for understanding and dialogue. Our two traditions are so related that they cannot ignore each other. Mutual knowledge must be encouraged at every level. There is evident in particular a painful ignorance of the history and traditions of Judaism, of which only negative aspects and often caricature seem to form part of the stock ideas of many Christians.

That is what these notes aim to remedy. This would mean that the Council text and *"Guidelines and Suggestions"* would be more easily and faithfully put into practice.

Johannes Cardinal Willebrands
President

Pierre Duprey
Vice-President

Jorge Meija
Secretary

---

*We continue to use the expression *Old Testament* because it is traditional (cf. already 2 Cor 3:14) but also because "Old" does not mean "out of date" or "out-worn". In any case, it is the *permanent* value of the O.T. as a source of Christian Revelation that is emphasized here (cf. *Dei Verbum*, 3).

**A man of gnostic tendency who in the second century rejected the Old Testament and part of the New as the work of an evil god, a demiurge. The Church reacted strongly against this heresy (cf. Irenaeus).

Other Volumes in This Series

Leon Klenicki, editor, *Toward A Theological Encounter* (A Stimulus Book, 1991).

John Rousmaniere, *A Bridge to Dialogue: The Story of Jewish-Christian Relations,* edited by James A. Carpenter and Leon Klenicki (A Stimulus Book, 1991).

Michael E. Lodahl, *Shekhinah/Spirit* (A Stimulus Book, 1992).

George M. Smiga, *Pain and Polemic: Anti-Judaism in the Gospels* (A Stimulus Book, 1992).

Eugene J. Fisher, editor, *Interwoven Destinies: Jews and Christians Through the Ages* (A Stimulus Book, 1993).

Anthony Kenny, *Catholics, Jews and the State of Israel* (A Stimulus Book, 1993).

Bernard J. Lee, SM, *Jesus and the Metaphors of God: The Christs of the New Testament,* Conversation on the Road Not Taken, Vol. 2 (A Stimulus Book, 1993).

Eugene J. Fisher, editor, *Visions of the Other: Jewish and Christian Theologians Assess the Dialogue* (A Stimulus Book, 1995).

Leon Klenicki and Geoffrey Wigoder, editors, *A Dictionary of the Jewish-Christian Dialogue,* Expanded Edition (A Stimulus Book, 1995).

Vincent Martin, *A House Divided: The Parting of the Ways between Synagogue and Church* (A Stimulus Book, 1995).

Philip A. Cunningham and Arthur F. Starr, editors, *Sharing Shalom: A Process for Local Interfaith Dialogue Between Christians and Jews* (A Stimulus Book, 1998).

Frank E. Eakin, Jr., *What Price Prejudice? Christian Antisemitism in America* (A Stimulus Book, 1998).

Ekkehard Schuster and Reinhold Boschert-Kimmig, *Hope Against Hope: Johann Baptist Metz and Elie Wiesel Speak Out on the Holocaust* (A Stimulus Book, 1999).

Mary C. Boys, *Has God Only One Blessing? Judaism as a Source of Christian Understanding* (A Stimulus Book, 2000).

Avery Dulles, SJ, and Leon Klenicki, editors, *The Holocaust, Never to Be Forgotten: Reflections on the Holy See's Document* We Remember (A Stimulus Book, 2000).

Johannes Reuchlin, *Recommendation Whether to Confiscate, Destroy and Burn All Jewish Books: A Classic Treatise against Anti-Semitism,* translated, edited, and with an introduction by Peter Wortsman (A Stimulus Book, 2000).

Philip A. Cunningham, *A Story of Shalom: The Calling of Christians and Jews by a Covenanting God* (A Stimulus Book, 2001).

Philip A. Cunningham, *Sharing the Scriptures,* The Word Set Free, Vol. 1 (A Stimulus Book, 2003).

Dina Wardi, *Auschwitz: Contemporary Jewish and Christian Encounters* (A Stimulus Book, 2003).

Michael Lotker, *A Christian's Guide to Judaism* (A Stimulus Book, 2004).

Lawrence Boadt and Kevin di Camillo, editors, *John Paul II in the Holy Land: In His Own Words: With Christian and Jewish Perspectives by Yehezkel Landau and Michael McGarry, CSP* (A Stimulus Book, 2005).

James K. Aitken and Edward Kessler, editors, *Challenges in Jewish-Christian Relations* (A Stimulus Book, 2006).

STIMULUS BOOKS are developed by the Stimulus Foundation, a not-for-profit organization, and are published by Paulist Press. The Foundation wishes to further the publication of scholarly books on Jewish and Christian topics that are of importance to Judaism and Christianity.

The Stimulus Foundation was established by an erstwhile refugee from Nazi Germany who intends to contribute with these publications to the improvement of communication between Jews and Christians.

Books for publication in this Series will be selected by a committee of the Foundation, and offers of manuscripts and works in progress should be addressed to:

The Stimulus Foundation
c/o Paulist Press
997 Macarthur Boulevard
Mahwah, NJ 07430
www.paulistpress.com